ICONS

DESIGN
HANDBOOK

Charlotte & Peter Fiell

DESIGN
HANDBOOK

CONCEPTS · MATERIALS · STYLES

TASCHEN

KÖLN LONDON LOS ANGELES MADRID PARIS TOKYO

*"Utility is one
of the principal
sources of beauty
... the fitness of
any system or
machine to pro-
duce the end for
which it was in-
tended, bestows
a certain propri-
ety and beauty
upon the whole,
and renders the
very thought and
contemplation of
it agreeable."*
Adam Smith,
*The Theory of the
Moral Sentiments*,
1759

Throughout its history, design has been intertwined with everyday life and culture. Its compass is vast, incorporating three-dimensional objects, graphics and integrated systems from information technology to urban environments. Defined most broadly as the conception and planning of all man-made products, design is ubiquitous. Design as we understand it today, however, is often traced to the birth of mechanized production during the Industrial Revolution. Before this, objects were made through craft production, where conception and realization were usually undertaken by an individual creator. The advent of industrial processes and the division of labour separated design from making. At the same time, design enjoyed no special status among the many interrelated aspects of mechanized manufacture. It was only through design reformers, such as William Morris, that it acquired theoretical and philosophical dimensions. As a result, the late nineteenth and early twentieth centuries witnessed an extraordinary flowering of design idealism in Europe from the **Arts and Crafts Movement**, to **Art Nouveau** and the **Jugendstil**. The thoroughgoing unification of design theory with industrial production came soon after, through the efforts of, among others, Walter Gropius. In an attempt both to reconcile social idealism with commercial reality, and to embrace the emerging industrial and technological culture, Gropius founded the **Bauhaus** in 1919. The principles forged there were subsequently promoted by the New Bauhaus in Chicago – later named the **Institute of Design** – and the **Hochschule für Gestaltung, Ulm**. The influential fusion of design and industrial civilisation that they propounded became known as the **Modern Movement** or the **International Style**. By the 1960s, however, this Modernist consensus had begun to fragment. The **Independent Group** in Britain, and the luminaries of **Anti-Design** and **Radical Design** in Italy dismantled Modernist nostrums, leading ultimately to **Pop Design**, **Deconstructivism** and **Post-Modernism**. In studying design history, it is important to remember that designs cannot be understood outside their social, economic, political, cultural and technological contexts. Patterns of consumer taste are forever altering. Designers and manufacturers react to rapidly changing imperatives of cost and demand. Indeed, even the economic cycles of Western economies have impacted on designers, as seen in the interrelationship of design and **styling**. While styling is concerned with the surface treatment of a product, design is primarily about problem solving. Design tends to be holistic in approach, generally seeking simplification and essentiality. Although styling is frequently a complementary element of a design solution, they are distinct disciplines. During economic downturns, **utilitarian design** usually predominates; in periods of prosperity, anti-rationalism is apt to flourish. Understanding the complexity of this history, and the diversity of design philosophies, also requires a knowledge of the design process and its increasing elaboration. For instance, design work for industrial production is often divided between numerous professionals: model makers, market researchers, materials specialists, engineers and production technicians. The designer can become obscured among this plethora of experts, each with their own vision. Equally, the corporate pursuit of competitive products can wield enormous influence over the work and careers of designers. Other designers, however, have chosen to operate independently, sidestepping the constraints of the industrial process and producing work concerned with self-expression. To this extent, design is not invariably intertwined with mechanized production, but is primarily a means of conveying ideas and values in accordance with individual, corporate, institutional or national objectives. The products of design, then, offer an insight into the character of the designer and his/her understanding of the relationship between the design solution, the consumer and the wider society. This handbook, therefore, aims to highlight the pluralism of design and its internal debates concerning such issues as: the role of technology and the industrial process; the primacy of simplicity and affordability over luxury and exclusivity; and the role of function, aesthetics, ornament and symbolism in objects for use. It features those concepts, movements, schools and institutions that have advanced the development of forms, materials applications and technical processes, and that have shaped the course of design theory and practice. From **Art Deco** to **Memphis,** they have influenced cultures, societies and notions of taste. Sections are also devoted to particular materials and their properties, such as **Bakelite**, **plywood** and **carbon fibre**; to less well-known areas of design practice, for instance **medical design**, **military design** and **design for sport**; and to specific design processes, for example **Computer-Aided Design**. The geographical remit has been limited largely to Europe and North America. The scope of the book demands selectivity, and the entries should be seen as broadly representative of the many different approaches to design. Entries are listed alphabetically with cross-references appearing in bold type so as to reveal illuminating linkages between concepts, movements and styles. In highlighting the plural nature of design, a further aim has been to demonstrate that the ideas and values transmitted by designers are conditional and not absolute. Design solutions are invariably ephemeral, as the needs of designers, manufacturers and consumers change. However, perhaps the key to diversity in design is the belief that even the most successful design solution can always be improved upon.

"Our capacity to go beyond the machine rests upon our power to assimilate the machine. Until we have absorbed the lessons of objectivity, impersonality, neutrality, the lesson of the mechanical realm, we cannot go further in our development toward the more richly organic, the more profoundly human."
Lewis Mumford, *Technics and Civilization*, 1934

AERODYNAMICS AESTHETIC MOVEME
DESIGN ANTHROPOMETRICS ANTI-DE
CRAFTS MOVEMENT (GB) ARTS & CR
BAKELITE BAUHAUS BENT WOOD BIC
FIBRE CERAMICS CHROMIUM CO
COMPUTER-AIDED DESIGN & -MANUF,
IDENTITY CRAFT REVIVAL DE STIJL DE
DESIGN FOR DISABILITY DESIGN FO
FOR THE THIRD WORLD DEUTSCHER
ERGONOMICS ESSENTIALISM FORDIS
KUNSTWERK GOOD DESIGN HIGH-TEC
INDEPENDENT GROUP INDUSTRIAL D
INTERNATIONAL STYLE JUGENDSTI
MILITARY DESIGN MINIATURIZATION M
DESIGN PACKAGING PLANNED OBS
DESIGN POST-INDUSTRIALISM POST-
RADICAL DESIGN RATIONALISM RE
RUBBER SECESSION SEMIOTICS SIGN,
DIZATION STREAMLINING STYLING S
TUBULAR METAL UTILITARIAN DESIG

AGITPROP ALUMINIUM ANONYMOUS

GN ART DECO ART NOUVEAU ARTS &

TS MOVEMENT (USA) AVANT-GARDE

ORPHISM BORAX BRANDING CARBON

UR IN DESIGN COMPASSO D'ORO

TURE CONSTRUCTIVISM CORPORATE

NSTRUCTIVISM DESIGN FOR CHILDREN

AFETY DESIGN FOR SPORT DESIGN

RKBUND ENVIRONMENTAL DESIGN

FUNCTIONALISM FUTURISM GESAMT-

HOCHSCHULE FÜR GESTALTUNG, ULM

IGN INSTITUTE OF DESIGN, CHICAGO

KITSCH MEDICAL DESIGN MEMPHIS

DERN MOVEMENT MODERNE ORGANIC

ESCENCE PLASTICS PLYWOOD POP

ODERNISM PRODUCT ARCHITECTURE

RO DESIGN ROYAL COLLEGE OF ART

E SOFT DESIGN/SOFT-TECH STANDAR-

REALISM SWISS SCHOOL TAYLORISM

VKHUTEMAS WIENER WERKSTÄTTE

AERODYNAMICS

Aerodynamics is a branch of physics concerned with the study of air and liquid motion and the forces that act on a body, such as an aeroplane, car or ship, when it passes through such media. It is based on the fundamental principle that the less resistance, the faster and more efficiently a body can move. The fact that air resists rather than impels the movement of a projectile was already recognised in the late 15th century by such pioneering engineers as Leonardo da Vinci. Astronomer and mathematician Galileo Galilei subsequently demonstrated that resistance was proportional to the velocity of an object. In the late 17th century, the Dutch physicist Christiaan Huygens and the British mathematician and physicist Sir Isaac Newton established that the resistance acting on the motion of a body was proportional to the square of its velocity. These and other subsequent discoveries into the nature of aerodynamics provided the scientific basis for the eventual practical application of aerodynamics to the design of ships, trains, automobiles, aircraft and rockets. Modern aerodynamics emerged around the time of the Wright brothers' first powered flight in 1903. The German physicist Ludwig Prandtl is generally acknowledged as the father of this modern science; it was his discovery, in 1904, of the boundary layer which adjoins the surface of a body moving in air or water, which led to a greater understanding of drag forces. Prandtl and the British engineer Frederick Lanchester later independently

Alfa Romeo 40–60 HP, 1913

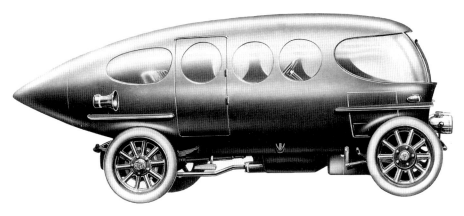

worked on wing theory, which explained the principles of airflow and the concept of lift. By the start of the 1920s, industrial designers such as Paul Jaray were employing wind tunnels to develop better and more efficient aerodynamic designs. In demonstrating that the reduction of drag through aerodynamic **streamlining** increased speed, reduced fuel consumption and improved stability, Jaray's findings had a profound impact upon automobile design, as evident particularly in the case of cars produced by Tatra, Audi and Porsche. Many of the streamlined forms of the 1930s, were driven purely by stylistic concerns, however, rather than by scientific data or – in the case of such domestic appliances as vacuum cleaners and refrigerators – by any real need for aerodynamic performance at all. An exception was Chrysler's *Airflow* automobile designed by Carl Breer in 1934, which although not a commercial success, was a remarkably advanced and influential de-sign. Other prominent pioneers of aerodynamics include the Hungarian-born engineer Theodor von Kármán, whose research led to major advances in turbulence theory and supersonic flight.

Auto Union (AUDI)
Type C racing car
with streamlined
racing body,
1936–1937

AESTHETIC MOVEMENT

Thomas Jeckyll,
Sunflower andiron
for Barnard, Bishop
& Barnard, c. 1880

The Aesthetic Movement evolved out of a previous art movement in Britain, which had combined the Gothic and Queen Anne Revivals. These earlier styles were interwoven with Eastern influences, by Bruce Talbert and Thomas Jeckyll among others, so as to create a hybrid Anglo-Oriental style. Inspired by Japanese woodcuts as well as the Oriental and Middle Eastern wares imported by companies such as Liberty & Co., Aesthetic Movement designers, including E. W. Godwin and Christopher Dresser, sought to reform design by adopting pure uncluttered lines. Aestheticism became a "lifestyle" choice for the progressive middle classes, such as those residing in Bedford Park in West London, and Liberty & Co. disseminated the style not only through their household furnishings but also through the marketing of loose and flowing Aesthetic clothes for women. James Abbot McNeill Whistler and Thomas Jeckyll's "Peacock Room" for F. R. Leyland's London residence (1876–1877) – now in the Freer Gallery, Washington – shows the Aesthetic Movement at its most exotic. The greatest proponents of Aestheticism were undoubtedly Oscar Wilde and Aubrey Beardsley who glorified the doctrine of "art for art's sake" in the heady *fin-de-siècle* era. The Aesthetic Movement, which was symbolized by the sunflower motif, also manifested itself in the United States, most notably in the work of the Herter Brothers and Louis Comfort Tiffany, and in France in the work of François-Eugène Rousseau. The Aesthetic Movement had some influence on two quite separate design movements: **Art Nouveau** through its use of motifs taken from nature and the **Modern Movement** through its adoption of abstracted Japanese forms.

AGITPROP

RUSSIA

The term Agitprop derives from the Russian phrase *agitatsiya propaganda* – "agitation propaganda" – that was put forth by Vladimir I. Lenin as an aspect of Communist doctrine in which the strategies of agitation and propaganda were blended to achieve political victory. Agitation was defined as the use of political slogans and half-truths to stir the masses into confronting their grievances, while propaganda was defined as the promotion of historical and scientific arguments to politically sway the intelligentsia. Following the Russian revolution in 1917, the Communist Party set up the *Agitprobyuro* (Bureau of

Sergei Vasilievich Chekhonin, propaganda plate for the State Porcelain Factory in Petrograd, 1919

Agitation and Propaganda) for the development of state-sponsored Soviet art and design, which subsequently became known as Agitprop. Using pre-Revolution blanks, designers such as Sergei Vasilievich Chekhonin, Kasimir Malevich, Maria Vasilievna Lebedeva and Nikolai Suetin decorated porcelain with slogans and motifs found on political posters and rally decorations. For the Revolution's first anniversary, Futurist Agitprop buildings and monuments were designed by Natan Altman for St. Peterburg's Uritskii Square. A year later, in 1919, Vasilii Ermilov took part in several Agitprop projects for posters, train decorations and interiors of clubs. Agitprop was intended to drum up popular support for the Revolution, and its grandiose schemes, such as Vladimir Tatlin's famous Constructivist structure *Pamiatnik III emu Internatsionalu* (Monument to the Third International) of 1919–1920 in Petrograd, reflected the desire for a new world order.

ALUMINIUM

Rodney Kinsman,
Seville bench for
OMK, 1991

Aluminium is the most abundantly found metallic element in the Earth's crust (forming up to 8 % by weight) and is the world's most widely used non-ferrous metal. Although it never occurs in its metallic form in nature, its compounds are present to some extent in nearly all rocks. The principle ore from which aluminium is extracted is bauxite, a mixture of hydrated aluminium oxides. Although unsuccessful in his attempt, in 1807, to extract the metal, it was Humphrey Davy who gave it the name "aluminum" – a

Ernest Race,
BA chair for Race
Furniture, 1945 –
made from re-
smelted aluminium
scrap

name that was retained in Canada and the United States but modified to "aluminium" in England and many other countries. A crude form of aluminium was eventually isolated in 1825 by the Danish chemist Hans Christian Ørsted. Introduced to the public in 1855 at the Paris Exposition, aluminium was initially only available in small quantities and was very expensive. In 1886, however, following the advent of relatively plentiful and cheap electric power, the commercial method of producing aluminium was simultaneously discovered by the American Charles Martin Hall and the Frenchman Paul Louis Toussaint Héroult. Their electrolytic process made low-priced aluminium available for the first time, and annual production rose dramatically – from around only 17 tonnes in 1886 to a massive 7,200 tonnes by 1900. In the 1930s aluminium became the material of choice for many industrial designers, especially in America, as its inherent properties suited the prevalent taste for smooth streamlined surfaces. Lightweight, ductile, highly malleable, non-toxic, corrosion-resistant and an excellent conductor of heat and electricity, applications of aluminium ranged from kitchenware to aircraft. Aluminium alloys can be cast, pressed, machined, rolled into a thin foil, spun and even extruded into tubes and other hollow forms. Aluminium can also be mixed with materials such as manganese to produce a metal alloy that is equal in strength to steel. In terms of industrial production, aluminium remains the most favoured metal; with increasingly sophisticated casting and extrusion technology, it continues to find new and highly innovative applications from furniture to highly engineered mechanical components.

Yoshinori Ive,
Ultegra group set
6500 bicycle
components
for Shimano,
1997–1998

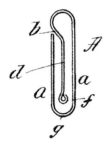

Fig.2.

ANONYMOUS DESIGN

Early design for a
paperclip

Six anonymous
designs – from
the humble screw
to the handy safety
pin

Many product designs that we take for granted in our daily
lives have evolved anonymously over decades or even centuries, through a process of "natural selection" that is driven
by practical need rather than by aesthetic concern. Objects
such as these are often superlatively functional, as their performance has been honed by successive generations of designers, craftsmen and manufacturers. The designer Gio Ponti described these types of
objects as "designs without adjectives" as they belong to no particular style
or movement. As early as the mid-19th century, anonymous designs were
being praised for their honesty, integrity and beauty – at a meeting of the
Freemasons of the Church in London in 1849, William Smith Williams stated
that: "The adaptation of the thing for its purpose, so far from producing ug-
liness, tends to beauty. ... In the commonest, rudest, and oldest implements
of husbandry – the plough, the scythe, the sickle – we have examples of

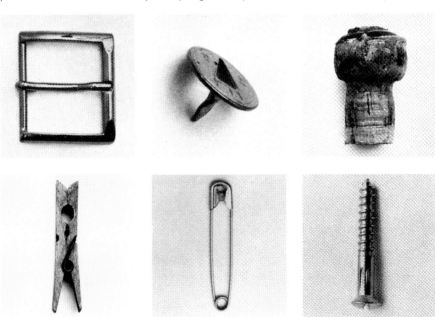

beautiful curves. The most elementary and simple of forms, if well-proportioned and of graceful contour, are the most pleasing." Similar sentiments were later taken up by the **Deutscher Werkbund**, which illustrated industrially produced and highly functional anonymous products in its catalogue *Form ohne Ornament* (Form without Ornament) of 1924. The classic English teapot sometimes known as the "Brown Betty" is an example of a remarkably functional anonymous design. Having evolved over hundreds of years, this teapot pours well, brews tea beautifully and does not stain – few designs can claim superior fitness for purpose. The study of anonymous designs, such as the paperclip, the clothes peg, the champagne cork, the wine bottle, the zip fastener, the thumb tack, the safety pin, the padlock, tweezers and the wood screw, has highlighted the fact that an evolutionary rather than revolutionary approach to design more often than not produces the best solutions.

"Brown Betty" teapot, England – a design type that has been in existence for centuries

ANTHROPOMETRICS

Anthropometric
chart, c. 1960s

"Joe" – the average
man, from Henry
Dreyfuss' book,
Designing for People,
1955

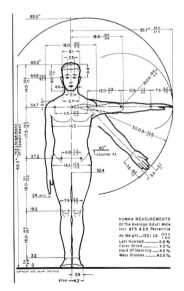

HUMAN MEASUREMENTS
Of The Average Adult Male
Incl. 97.5 & 2.5 Percentile
Av. Weight....153.1 Lb.
Left Handed _____ 6.6%
Color Blind _____ 3.5%
Hard Of Hearing _____ 4.5%
Wear Glasses _____ 43.6%

Anthropometrics is the systematic collection and correlation of measurements of the human body. Having originated in the late 19th century with social scientists evaluating the physical differences between racial groups and attempting to establish evidence of criminal physical types, anthropometrics did not become a factor in design until the 1920s, when pioneering Scandinavian designers such as Kaare Klint began relating the dimensional aspects of the human form to the design of everyday objects. Also known in the United States as "human engineering", the application of anthropometric data became more common after the Second World War, when wartime research was made public. The American industrial designer Henry Dreyfuss was one the most important proponents of anthropometrics and the closely related field of **ergonomics** as essential tools for designers. His seminal *Designing for People* (1955) features scale drawings of "Mr & Mrs Average" (whom Dreyfuss christened "Joe" and "Josephine"), which illustrate numerous average measurements between physical "landmarks", such as the distance between the wrist and elbow, and the knee and ankle. Dreyfuss described how he used maquettes of Joe and Josephine to determine the optimum layouts of product designs ranging from tractors seats to telephone control consoles. Dreyfuss elaborated on his extensive anthropometric researches in his later book, *The Measure of Man: Human Factors in Design* (1960), which helped establish the application of anthropometric data as standard practice in the design community. Dreyfuss' research into anthropometrics was later developed by Scandinavian design groups such as Ergonomi Design Gruppen, which concentrated on **design for disability**. The application of anthropometric data in design planning has in recent years been greatly assisted by the use of advanced computer software and is now widely used in most areas of design, from transportation and furniture to communications and clothing.

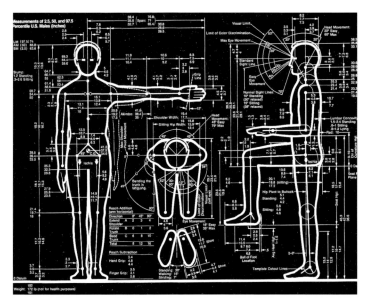

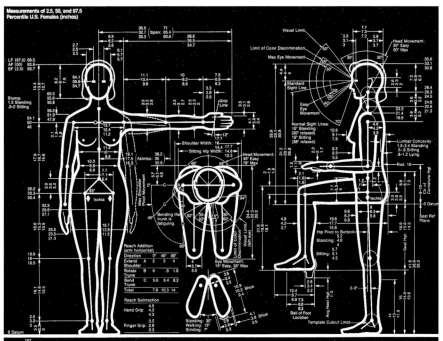

Diagrams showing percentile measurements of males and females in the United States from Henry Dreyfuss Associates' *Humanscale* publication

ANTI-DESIGN

Rejecting the rational precepts of the **Modern Movement**, Anti-Design attempts to validate individual creative expression within design. **Surrealism** was one of the first conscious examples of Anti-Design and influenced the 1940s Turinese Baroque style of Anti-Rationalist designers such as Carlo Mollino. Anti-Design did not, however, become an **avant-garde** force until the late 1960s when several **Radical Design** groups were formed in Italy. These groups, such as Archizoom, Superstudio, UFO, Gruppo Strum and 9999, believed that Modernism was no longer attuned to the avant-garde

Piero Gatti, Cesare Paolini & Franco Teodoro, *Sacco* beanbag for Zanotta, 1968

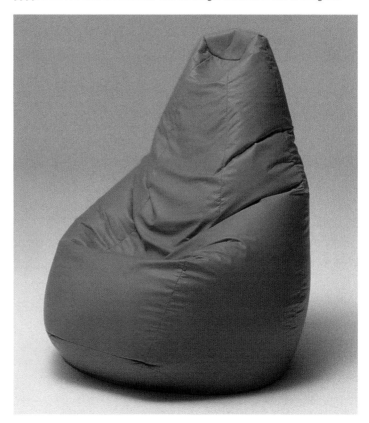

Alessandro Mendini,
Kandissi sofa for
Studio Alchimia,
1978

and was no longer a cultural driving force, having been subverted by industrial interests into a blatantly consumerist marketing ploy. Highly critical of advanced technology and consumerism, the Anti-Design movement propounded the "design of evasion" and sought to demonstrate through provocative projections, such as Superstudio's super structures and Archizoom's *No-Stop City*, that if rationalism was taken too far it became absurd. In 1974, Global Tools, a school of counter-architecture and design, was officially founded to explore simple non-industrial techniques in an attempt to promote individual creativity. A year later, Global Tools was disbanded, marking the end of the first Anti-Design phase of the 1970s. At this time it seemed to many designers associated with the movement, such as Alessandro Mendini and Ugo La Pietra, that there was no future for radical counter-design. Within three years, however, the Anti-Design crusade was taken up again by others aligned to Studio Alchimia, who rejected the prevailing conservatism of the mid-1970s and sought to bring spontaneity, creativity and meaning back into design. At Studio Alchimia, the functional concerns of design were supplanted by political content, ironic quotations from mass-culture and knowing references to past styles. Studio Alchimia claimed that "there is a need today for distant, very distant objects to be situated among men and in the world as signals of our vocation to the magic of thought, like lifebuoys in the stormy sea of modernity. Paradoxical, unique, isolated, complete and self-defined objects". In the early 1980s, with the emergence of **Memphis** in Italy and with American critics of Modernism such as Charles Jencks, who called for "elements which are hybrid rather than pure ... messy vitality over obvious unity" (M. Collins & A. Papadakis, *Post-Modern Design*, London 1989, p. 49), coming to the fore, Anti-Design, with its liberation of decoration for its own sake, evolved into a recognizable international style – **Post-Modernism**. During the boom years of the 1980s, Anti-Design made significant inroads into mainstream design with many consumers putting designer label cachet above all other considerations.

Alessandro Mendini, *Zabro* chair/table for Zanotta, 1984

ART DECO

Edgar-William Brandt, *La Tentation* floor lamp, c. 1925 (base by E.-W. Brandt, shade by Daum Frères)

Art Deco was an international decorative style, rather than a design movement, which emerged in Paris during the 1920s. Prior to this, elements of the style had already appeared in the work of the **Wiener Werkstätte**, the Italian furniture designer Carlo Bugatti and the Russian Constructivists. Taking over from the turn-of-the-century **Art Nouveau**, which with its ahistorical bearing looked to natural forms, Art Deco drew its stylistic references from an eclectic range of sources including ancient Egyptian civilization, tribal art, **Surrealism**, **Futurism**, **Constructivism**, Neo-Classicism, geometric abstraction, popular culture and the **Modern Movement**. Leading exponents of the new style, such as Jacques-Émile Ruhlmann, espoused for the most part the ideal of superlative craftsmanship and incorporated exotic woods and luxury materials such as shagreen and mother-of-pearl in their designs. Its reliance on private patronage, most notably from the French couturiers, Paul Poiret and Jacques Doucet, and its incompatibility with industrialized production ensured that Art Deco was a relatively short-lived style, inevitably overtaken by more progressive approaches to design. The "Exposition Internationale des Arts Décoratifs et Industriels Modernes", held in Paris in 1925, included Le Corbusier's Pavillon de l'Esprit Nouveau as well as Ruhlmann's Hôtel du Collectionneur and exhibits by other well-known Art Deco designers such as Pierre-Émile Legrain. It was from the title of this landmark exhibition that the term Art Deco was eventually coined. From the beginning, the Art Deco style spanned the work of designers such as René Lalique, Jean Dunand, and Edgar-William Brandt as well as the creations of modernists such as Eileen Gray, Pierre Chareau and Robert Mallet-Stevens. Indeed, even designers closely associated with the Modern Movement, such as Le Corbusier and Jean Prouvé, were at times inspired by the sumptuousness of Art Deco. After 1925 the style was expressed in the work of many designers, not only in France and continental Europe but increasingly in Britain and the United States. It was particularly well received in America where designs such as Paul Frankl's *Skyscraper* furniture and William van Alen's Chrysler Building (1928–1930) in New York – perhaps the ultimate expres-

sion of Art Deco architecture – were seen to encapsulate the aspirations of the nation. In Britain, the Art Deco style was more subdued than elsewhere and was subtly expressed in the architecture and product design of Wells Coates. The style was also frequently used in Britain for cinemas, especially those owned by Odeon, which projected inside the silver-screen world of Art Deco boudoirs and Hollywood-style chromed glamour. During the 1930s, the style became increasingly popular owing to its associations with this dreamlike Hollywood lifestyle and, as a result, was eventually fully embraced by mainstream manufacturers. Although **Bakelite** had been developed in America in 1907, it was not until the late 1920s that this thermoset plastic became a viable material for large-scale mass-production. The sculptural Art Deco style was eminently suited to the moulding requirements of this new medium and during the 1930s Art Deco radio casings, together with a plethora of other Bakelite objects, were mass produced. The Art Deco style, however, became increasingly debased with the production of **Kitsch** objects that had little in common with the superior craftsmanship of earlier French

Jean Dunand,
snake vase, c. 1913

Art Deco objects. Eventually, the style was curtailed by the advent of the Second World War when its essential reliance on decoration and its maximalist aesthetic could no longer be sustained. In the 1960s, Art Deco began to enjoy a reappraisal both on the collectors' market and among young designers disillusioned with Modernism. During the 1980s, post-modern designers such as Robert Venturi, Hans Hollein and Charles Jencks paid homage to Art Deco through their own idiosyncratic work which, like that of their antecedents, revelled in excess and exuberance.

ART NOUVEAU

Art Nouveau was an ahistorical style that emerged during the 1880s. It was inspired by the earlier British **Arts & Crafts Movement**, which was sometimes known as the "New Art". During the 1890s, Charles Rennie Mackintosh and designers associated with the Vienna **Secession**, such as Josef Maria Olbrich, introduced abstracted naturalistic forms to design that were curvilinear while others, such as Hermann Obrist and August Endell, pioneered the use of whiplash motifs. One of the greatest exponents of Art Nouveau was the Belgian architect Victor Horta, whose Hôtel Tassel (1892–1893) was one of the first expressions of the style in architecture. This residential project innovatively incorporated ironwork as both a structural and decorative device, and the designer's use of stem-like columns that branch into swirling tendrils led to the coining of the term "Horta Line". Similarly, in France, the style became known as "Style Guimard" in recognition of the writhing and intertwined forms employed by

Émile Gallé, cameo vase with autumn crocus decoration, 1899

Friedrich Adler, coffee service for Metallwarenfabrik Orion, 1904

Hector Guimard – most, notably for his cast-iron entrances to the Paris Métro (c. 1900). There, the term "Le Style Moderne" was also used to identify Art Nouveau, while in Germany the name **Jugendstil** was adopted. In Spain, especially in Catalonia, the Art Nouveau style flourished through the work of Antonio Gaudí y Cornet and his followers. They generally referred to Art Nouveau as "Modernisme" while in Italy the term "Stile Liberty" was coined in recognition of the role played by the London department store Liberty & Co. in the promotion of the style. Émile Gallé and other designers associated with the École de Nancy produced notable furniture and glassware in the Art Nouveau style. The sinuous lines and the elongation of floral

forms, which readily identify Art Nouveau, were directly inspired by the natural world rather than past styles. Indeed, the abstracted and bulbous forms of Louis Comfort Tiffany's Favrile vases capture the very essence of nature. The reason designers of the 1890s looked to nature for inspiration had much to do with earlier scientific research into the workings of the natural world such as Charles Darwin's treatise *On the Origin of Species*, published in 1859, the botanical illustrations of Ernst Haeckel and the exquisite photographic flower studies taken by Karl Blossfeldt in the late 19th century. With its outright rejection of historicism, Art Nouveau can be considered the first truly modern international style. It became inextricably linked to the decadence of the *fin-de-siècle*, however, owing to its reliance on ornamental motifs. As a result, it was

Eugène Gaillard,
pedestal for
J. P. Christophe,
c. 1901–1902

Paul Hankar, "New England" shopfront in Brussels, c. 1900

→**Victor Horta**, Interior of the Hôtel Tassel in Brussels, 1893

overtaken stylistically in the early 20th century by the machine aesthetic and the **avant-garde**'s preference for simple geometric forms better suited to industrial production.

ARTS & CRAFTS MOVEMENT

GREAT BRITAIN

Walter Crane, *The Orange Tree* textile for Jeffrey & Co., 1902 (reissued by Arthur Sanderson & Sons)

The British Arts & Crafts Movement comprised a loose collaboration of progressive architects and designers whose aim was to reform design and ultimately society through a return to handcraft. Appalled by the social and environmental consequences of industrialization and by the plethora of overly decorated, poor quality machine-made products, designers in the mid-19th century such as William Morris led a crusade against the age in which they lived and advocated a simpler and more ethical approach to design and manufacture. Their distrust of industrial production, which had turned skilled craftsman into "wage slaves", led to efforts to re-invigorate the traditional crafts through the design and execution of high quality wares that were not only useful but also beautiful. The first phase of the British Arts & Crafts Movement was influenced by the Pre-Raphaelite Brotherhood and the medieval escapism it popularized – the artists, Dante Gabriel Rossetti, Edward Burne-Jones and Ford Madox Brown all designed for Morris & Co. – and by late Gothic Revivalism, as practised by the architect George Edmund Street. Of greatest influence, however, were the reforming ideas of Augustus Pugin and John Ruskin, while William Morris was among the first to attempt to put many of their theories into practice when he established Morris, Marshall & Faulkner & Co. in 1861 (changed to Morris & Co. in 1874). Morris & Co.'s products did not embrace mechanized production methods but instead espoused the inherent simplicity of vernacularism and the honesty of handcraftsmanship. Rather than attempting to reform industrial production, which was driven by commerce, the early proponents of the Arts & Crafts Movement sought to promote democracy and social cohesion through craft. Working within a rampantly capitalist society, Morris was a committed socialist who had a utopian vision in which handcraft offered moral salvation to both workers and consumers. He was most concerned by the compartmentalization of the industrial process, for through the division of labour, the worker's well-being and the arts as a whole were undermined. Morris could only accept mechanization if it produced objects of quality and reduced workers' burdens, rather than just increasing productivity. The paradox was that the handcrafted products of Morris & Co. and others were costly to produce and could only be afforded by the wealthiest members of society. Inspired by both Morris and Ruskin's advocacy of morality in design and their belief in the social importance of craft and community, the second phase Arts & Crafts designers, William R. Lethaby, Arthur Heygate Mackmurdo and Charles R. Ashbee, founded organizations such as The Century Guild (1882), the St George's Art Society (1883) and the Art Workers' Guild (1884) to produce objects of reformed design. The term "Arts & Crafts" was not coined until 1888 when members of the Art Workers' Guild formed the Arts & Crafts Exhibition Society. Though second phase Arts & Crafts designers increasingly embraced vernacularism, some such as Charles Voysey and Ashbee concluded that Morris' vision of widely available well-designed products was unattainable without mechanization. Ashbee, who founded the Guild of Handicraft in 1888, even went so far as to accuse Morris, with his preoccupation with the past and near total rejection of machine production, of "intellectual Luddism". It was Ashbee, however, who came the closest to realizing the Movement's dream of a "rural ideal" when he moved his Guild of Handicraft to Chipping Campden in 1902. The Arts & Crafts Movement had by then close associations with the Cotswolds through Ernest Gimson and

Charles Voysey, woven textile, c. 1900

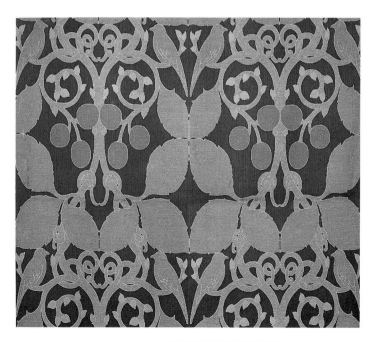

Sidney and Ernest Barnsley's working in Pinbury from the 1890s. From about 1910, Gordon Russell designed furniture in Broadway in the Arts & Crafts manner, yet by 1926 its production was largely mechanized in an ongoing attempt to reconcile high quality with affordability. Russell later oversaw the production of Utility furniture, and certainly the underlying morality of the Arts & Crafts Movement was central to the development of this state sponsored programme. Instrumental in the promotion of the Arts & Crafts style were Liberty & Co. and Heal & Sons, both of which had their own design studios and retailed Arts & Crafts furnishings and metalwork. Sometimes referred to as the "New Art", the second phase of the Arts & Crafts Movement can be seen to some extent as the British equivalent of the Continental **Art Nouveau** style and as such remained popular until the outbreak of war in 1914. The virtues of simplicity, utility and appropriateness that the Arts & Crafts Movement promoted, and its fundamental proposition that design could and should be used as a democratic tool for social change, were highly influential to the early pioneers of the **Modern Movement**. Throughout the 20th century, the Arts & Crafts idiom has survived through the work of designers allied to the **Craft Revival**.

Sidney Barnsley,
wardrobe, c. 1911

THE CRAFTSMAN

VOL. V   JANUARY·1904   NO.4

COPY 25 CENTS   PUBLISHED MONTHLY BY THE UNITED CRAFTS SYRACUSE·N·Y·-U·S·A·   YEAR 3 DOLLARS

Front cover of *The
Craftsman* magazine,
1904

ARTS & CRAFTS MOVEMENT

USA

Many American designers were inspired by the ideals of the British Arts & Crafts Movement and its demonstration in practice that a national style could be propagated through the espousal of traditional vernacular forms. William Morris' and Charles R. Ashbee's advocacy of rural artistic communities appealed to American designers such as Gustav Stickley, Charles P. Limbert and Elbert G. Hubbard who were seeking refuge from the increasing industrialization of their country. In 1898, Gustav Stickley visited Europe and while there met, among others, Charles R. Ashbee and Charles Voysey. On his return, Stickley established his own workshops in Syracuse, New York, and from 1901 began publishing his extremely influential magazine *The Craftsman*. While his rustic furniture designs looked back to the vernacular forms used in the pioneer days, he advocated honesty and simplicity in design believing that "decadence is the natural sequence of over refinement". American Arts & Crafts designs were in general less complicated in construction and less decorated than their British counterparts, for it was the underlying social and democratic aspects of the Movement rather than its emphasis on superlative craftsmanship that appealed to designers in the United States. The architect William L. Price, for instance, was so inspired by William Morris' utopian novel *News from Nowhere* (1889–1890) that he established the Rose Valley Community in Moylan, Philadelphia in 1901. This venture attempted to realize the Arts & Crafts ideal of a socially cohesive rural community in which members sought "joy through labour" and worked together to abolish social injustice. The social freedoms offered by the movement also attracted many women as it encouraged emancipation through its promotion of gender equality and female education. Many of the communities, however, were short lived due to the difficulties inherent in attempts at reconciling high quality handcraftsmanship with affordability. Only the Roycrofters community, established by Elbert G. Hubbard in 1893, was notable for its commercial success. In 1906, the Roycrofters workshops employed over four hundred craftsmen and the community even boasted an inn for tourists and potential customers. In California, architects and designers allied to the Arts & Crafts

Hugh Garden, *Teco* vase for the Gates Pottery, c. 1900

Movement were also inspired by the state's Spanish-Mexican heritage as well as Japanese Art and the Mission Style. Charles and Henry Greene eloquently fused these styles in their designs for wealthy clients' houses but their work differed significantly from Stickley's and Limbert's in that it incorporated exquisite detailing. Similarly, Frank Lloyd Wright, who was the greatest architect and designer to work within the Arts & Crafts idiom in the United States, synthesized Western and Eastern influences. His long and low Prairie School style of architecture combined with his skillful handling of natural materials enabled his buildings to blend in harmoniously with their surrounding environments. Wright's pioneering **Organic Design** bridged the Arts & Crafts Movement and the **Modern Movement** and in so doing greatly influenced later designers both in America and Europe.

AVANT-GARDE

The French term "avant-garde" refers to architects, designers, artists, writers and musicians, whose techniques and ideas are in advance of those generally known or accepted. Avant-garde design has traditionally made up only a small percentage of manufactured goods, yet its influence on the history of design has been enormous. Generally, such work has had an impact far beyond the circles of the minority audience for whom it was primarily intended, chiefly through media interest. For much of the 20th century, avant-garde de-

Gerrit Rietveld,
Red/Blue chair
(executed by G. van
de Groenekan,
1918–1923)

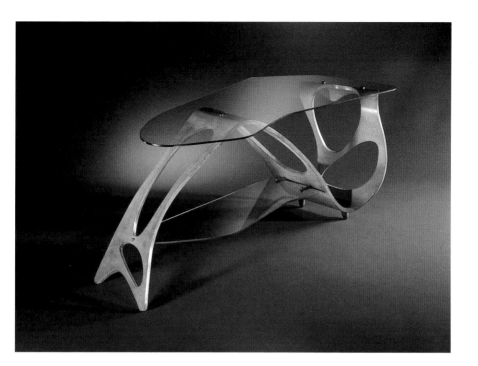

Carlo Mollino,
Arabesque table for
Apelli & Varesio,
1950

signers have remained outside the industrial mainstream owing to the limited appeal of their work and it has taken sometimes many years for more widely held tastes and attitudes to catch up. Marcel Breuer's pioneering **tubular metal** furniture from the late 1920s and early 1930s, for instance, was not nearly as widely accepted in its own day as it was in the 1960s and 70s. The avant-garde necessarily leads fashion, and styles are created in its wake. Post-war **Organic Design**, for example, stylistically influenced 1950s **Biomorphism**. The work of the avant-garde is frequently given the adjective "New" – New Art, **Art Nouveau**, New Wave – to describe its forward-looking agenda, and it is fair to say that the majority of the most important theoretical and practical innovations in 20th century design have been the direct result of avant-garde talent and vision.

BAKELITE

Isamu Noguchi, *Radio Nurse* nursery monitor for Zenith Radio Corporation, 1937 – with Bakelite housing

Leo Baekeland in his laboratory

The Belgian-born chemist and entrepreneur Leo Baekeland emigrated to America in 1889. His first invention was Velox, a photographic paper that could be developed in artificial light rather than in just natural light, which made its processing much more convenient for photographers. The rights to Velox were purchased for the then astronomical sum of $1,000,000 by George Eastman, who went on to rename his company the Eastman Kodak Company in 1902. The now wealthy Baekeland moved his family to the sumptuous Snug Rock estate near Yonkers, where he converted a barn into a laboratory. Around this time, the price of shellac – a resinous natural plastic, derived from the secretion of the *Laccifer Lacca* beetle in Southern Asia and used as an electrical insulator – began to increase dramatically as demand far outstripped supply. This prompted Baekeland and other chemists to begin searching for a synthetic alternative. Some 30 years earlier, in 1872, the German research chemist Adolf von Baeyer had succeeded in producing a synthetic horn-like resin from a reaction between phenol and formaldehyde. Baekeland now attempted to develop a more sophisticated synthetic insulating material, one that could be dissolved in solvents to produce a varnish, but that could also be moulded just like rubber. From 1904 he experimented tirelessly until he had developed a substance that he referred to as Bakelite – a synthetic resin formed from the chemical combination of phenols and formaldehydes. This early thermoset plastic was manufactured using a heated iron vessel known as a "bakelizer", which accurately controlled the phenol-formaldehyde reaction. After patenting this remarkable material, Baekeland began the commercial production of Bakelite – the world's first completely synthetic plastic – in 1909. A hard, infusible and chemically resistant plastic, Bakelite soon became known as "the material of a thousand uses". It was moulded into casings for telephones, cameras and pens, and into single-form prod-

ucts such as buttons, ashtrays and mixing bowls. As an excellent non-con-
ductor of electricity, Bakelite was particularly useful for electrical appliances,
especially radios and fans. Significantly, the advent of Bakelite made possible, for the first time, the large-scale mass production of many different
types of consumer products. Thanks to this and its suitability to the moulding process, Bakelite proceeded to change the aesthetic of many industrially
manufactured products. The streamlined and sculptural plastic forms of
many of the housewares manufactured in the 1930s would have been incon-
ceivable without the development of Bakelite. Phenol-formaldehyde resins,
including Bakelite, continue to be used as adhesives and paint additives in
many industrial applications, and are indispensable in the manufacture of
chemical equipment, machine and instrument housings, bottle closures,
electrical components and insulators. Leo Baekeland's revolutionary material not only heralded the "Age of Plastics" but also ensured that **plastics** became *the* materials of the 20th century.

BAUHAUS

1919–1933
WEIMAR, DESSAU & BERLIN, GERMANY

Although Walter Gropius was put forward for the directorship of the Kunstgewerbeschule at Weimar, which had been founded by Henry van de Velde in 1908, it closed before he could take up the position in 1915. Gropius maintained his contacts, however, at Weimar's other art school, the Hochschule für Bildende Kunst. As a soldier during the First World War, Gropius became anti-capitalist, his sympathies lying more with the craft ideals of the Helgar workshops than with the **Deutscher Werkbund** and its belief in industrial production. While at the front, Gropius formulated his "Proposals for the establishment of an educational institution to provide artistic advisory services to industry, trade and craft". In January 1916, his recommendations for the merging of the Kunstgewerbeschule and the Hochschule für Bildende Kunst into a single interdisciplinary school of craft and design were sent to the Großherzogliches Sächsisches Staatsministerium. In April 1919, Gropius was duly appointed director of the new Staatliches Bauhaus in Weimar and that same year the Bauhaus Manifesto was published. The Bauhaus, which means "building house", sought to reform educational theory and, in so doing, bring unity to the arts. For Gropius, construction or "making" was an important social, symbolic and intellectual endeavour and this sentiment pervaded Bauhaus teaching. The curriculum included a one-year preliminary course where students were taught the basic principles of design and colour theory. After completing this foundation year, students entered the various workshops situated in two buildings and trained in at least one craft. These workshops were intended to be self-supporting, relying on private commissions. The tutors were known as "masters" and some of them were members of local guilds, while the students were referred to as "apprentices". During the Bauhaus' first year, Gropius appointed three artists: Johannes Itten, who was responsible for the preliminary course, Lyonel Feininger and Gerhard Marcks. These tutors were joined by other Expressionists – Georg Muche at the end of 1919, Paul Klee and Oskar Schlemmer in 1921 and Wassily Kandinsky in 1922. During the earliest period of the Bauhaus, it was the charismatic Itten who played the most important role. Itten's classes,

Gyula Pap,
candelabra made in
the metal workshop
in Weimar,
1922–1923

which often commenced with breathing exercises and gymnastics, were
based on "intuition and method" or "subjective experience and objective
recognition". He believed that materials should be studied so as to unveil
their intrinsic qualities and encouraged his students to make inventive constructions from *objets trouvés*. Itten also taught theories of form, colour and
contrast as well as the appreciation of art history. In accord with Gropius,
Itten believed that natural laws existed for spatial composition just as they
did for musical composition and students were taught the importance of
elemental geometric forms such as the circle, square and cone. Like
Kandinsky, Itten attempted to reintroduce the spiritual to art. Both Itten and
Muche were highly involved with the Mazdaznan sect and tried to introduce
its teachings to the Bauhaus. Heads were shaved, loose monk-like garments
worn, a vegetarian diet with vast amounts of purifying garlic and regular
fastings adhered to, acupuncture and hot baths practised. However, this
Mazdaznan adventure into meditation and ritual undermined Gropius' authority and turned students against him. Eventually, conflict arose between
Gropius and Itten and the latter subsequently left in December 1922, mark-

ing the end of the Expressionist period at the Bauhaus. Josef Albers and László Moholy-Nagy were appointed as Itten's successors and although they followed the fundamental framework of his preliminary class, they rejected his ideologies for individual creative development and pursued a more industrial approach with students being taken on factory visits. Given Itten's bizarre teaching methods and the school's underlying socialist bearing, it is not surprising that, as a state institution, the Bauhaus attracted much political opposition in Weimar. The local authorities there, under pressure from local guilds who were concerned that work would be taken from their own members by Bauhaus students, demanded the staging of an exhibition so as to justify the State's continued support. The exhibition held in 1923 not only featured work from the Bauhaus but also included **De Stijl** designs such as Gerrit Rietveld's *Red/Blue chair* of 1918–1923. The influence of De Stijl on the

Lena Bergner, design for a bedroom carpet, 1928

→**Joost Schmidt,** poster for the Bauhaus Exhibition in Weimar, 1923

Bauhaus cannot be overstated, indeed Theo van Doesburg had lectured in Weimar. Another development seen at the 1923 exhibition was the new image that the Bauhaus forged for itself – the graphics from this period were self-consciously modern incorporating "New Typography", which was undoubtedly inspired by De Stijl and Russian **Constructivism**. Although this landmark exhibition received critical acclaim internationally, especially from the United States, it did not allay local fears. When Weimar became the first city in Germany to elect the National Socialist German Workers' Party, the school's grant was halved and in 1925 Gropius was forced to move the Bauhaus, which was by then regarded as a hotbed of communism and subversion. The school was relocated to Dessau where the ruling Social Democrats and the liberal mayor were far more politically receptive to its continuation and success. This industrial city, which was benefitting from the assistance loans from America made available by the Dawes Plan, offered the Bauhaus the financial support it so desperately needed. The aid was granted on the understanding that the school would part-fund itself through the production and retail of its designs. The amount of money offered meant that a new purpose-built school could be constructed and so, in 1926, the Staatliches Bauhaus moved into its newly completed Dessau headquarters, designed by Walter Gropius. In nearby woodland, a series of masters' houses of stark geometric design were constructed, which served as blueprints for future living. The Bauhaus Dessau building itself, with its highly rational pre-fabricated structure, marked an important turning point for the school from crafts towards industrial **Functionalism**. The masters were now referred to as professors and were no longer involved with the guilds while the school instituted the issuing of its own diplomas. By now, Gropius had become disillusioned with socialism and believed that Henry Ford's type of industrial capitalism could benefit workers and that in order to survive the Bauhaus needed to adopt an industrial approach to design. With the conviction that a better society could be created through the application of functionalism, Bauhaus designs were now conceived for industrial production and a machine aesthetic was consciously adopted. In November 1925, with the financial support of Adolf Sommerfeld, Gropius realized his long-held ambition of establishing a limited company to promote and retail the school's designs. Bauhaus GmbH duly produced a catalogue, designed by Herbert Bayer, which illustrated Bauhaus products. The sales of these

Marcel Breuer,
Lattenstuhl made
in the furniture
workshop in Weimar,
1922–1924

items were far from overwhelming, however. For the most part, this was no doubt due to the severity of the products' aesthetic but there was a further problem: though they appeared to be machine-made, the majority of the products were in fact unsuitable for industrial production. A few licensing agreements were drawn up between the Bauhaus and outside manufacturers but these did not bring in the revenues Gropius had hoped for. In 1928, Gropius tried to hand over the directorship of the Bauhaus to Ludwig Mies van der Rohe so that he could spend more of his time designing, but Mies refused. Eventually, the Swiss architect, Hannes Meyer, who had been appointed professor of the architecture department when it opened in April 1927, agreed to take over the position at the school, which by now was subtitled "Hochschule für Gestaltung" (Institute of Design). Meyer, who was a Communist, held the directorship until July 1930. He believed that form had to be governed by function and cost so that products would be both practical and affordable for working-class consumers. He attempted to introduce lectures on economics, psychology, sociology, biology and Marxism to the curriculum and closed the theatre workshop and reorganized the other workshops in an effort to rid the school of the costly "artiness" of previous years. During Meyer's tenure, the Bauhaus' approach to design became more scientific and the earlier Constructivist influence all but vanished. At this time, the Bauhaus also became more politicized with the school site being used as the focus for the political activities of a group of Marxist students. By 1930, there was a Communist cell of thirty-six students, which began to draw some unfavourable press. Upon the instigation of Gropius and Kandinsky, the city of Dessau authority fired Meyer when it was discovered he had provided funds for striking miners. Under pressure to de-politicize the Bauhaus for its own survival, Mies van der Rohe took over the directorship. He promptly closed the school, replaced its existing statutes, then re-opened it and forced the 170 students to re-apply. Five students who had been close to Meyer were expelled. A new curriculum was established with the preliminary course becoming non-compulsory. The study of architecture was given greater importance, which effectively turned the Bauhaus into a school of architecture. Although the applied art workshops continued, their remit was to supply only products that could be industrially manufactured. With Mies, architectural theory triumphed for a while over politics as he introduced, with his partner Lily Reich, the new apolitical programme of "Bau

Karl Hermann Haupt, design for a covered box, 1923

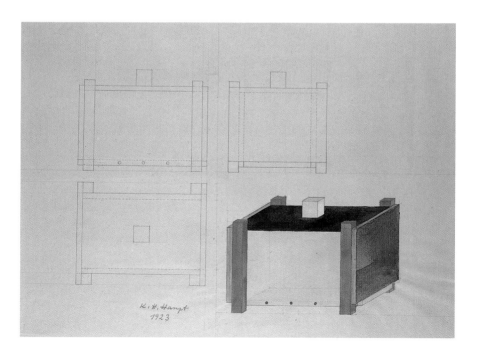

und Ausbau" (building and development). In October 1931, the National
Socialists, who had been pushing for the closure of the Bauhaus, swept to
power in Dessau winning 19 out of 36 seats and, on the 22nd August 1932,
a motion was passed for the closure of the school. The Bauhaus was subsequently re-established by Mies as a private school in Berlin but its political
past caught up with it when the National Socialists eventually seized power
in the city. The Gestapo raided the school's premises looking for incriminat-
ing communist literature and sealed the building, effectively closing it down.
On the 19th July 1933, the masters gathered together and voted to dissolve
the Bauhaus – formally marking the end of this truly remarkable institution.
Many of the masters, including Mies, Marcel Breuer, Walter Gropius, and
Josef Albers emigrated to the United States to escape persecution and in
1937 László Moholy-Nagy became the director of the short-lived New Bauhaus in Chicago. A year later, a retrospective of Bauhaus design was held
at the Museum of Modern Art, New York, and the school's reputation as
the most important design institution of the 20th century grew. The
Functionalist approach to design pioneered at the Bauhaus had a fundamental impact on subsequent industrial design practice and provided the

philosophical bedrock from which the **Modern Movement** evolved. The Bauhaus also had a profound and widespread impact on the way in which design was subsequently taught and this was most especially felt at the **Hochschule für Gestaltung, Ulm**.

Wilhelm Wagenfeld,
tea set for Jenaer
Glaswerke Schott &
Gen., 1931

BENT WOOD

Michael Thonet, *Model No. 14* armchair for Gebrüder Thonet, 1859

Adolf Loos, chair for the Café Museum for Jakob & Josef Kohn, c. 1898

The bending of solid wood for use in various applications has a long history. Egyptian furniture from as early as 2800 B.C., and the "klismos" chairs of ancient Greece may well have been constructed using this technique. By the 18th century, though, the practice had become widespread. Shipbuilders, coopers and wheelwrights all used bent wood, and carriage makers plunged wooden panels into hot sand to shape them. In England, bent wood was employed for the hoop back and arm rail of Windsor chairs, and in America the furniture-maker Samuel Gragg took this art to new levels of sophistication with his "elastic" chairs. The greatest strides in the production of bent wood furniture were, however, made by the Prussian designer and entrepreneur Michael Thonet. By the 1850s, Thonet's early experiments in the steam-bending of glued veneers had given way to designs in solid wood. A steady stream of beech planks arrived at the Gebrüder Thonet factory in Koritschan, Moravia, where they were cut into rods, lathe-turned and placed in a steam chamber at 100°C for between six and twenty-four hours. Exposed to heat and moisture the wood's oil and resin would partially dissolve, loosening its grain. Immediately on removal the rods were bent, clamped into cast-iron forms and placed in drying rooms. Alongside its distinct aesthetic potential, bent wood also offered Thonet considerable cost savings. The process was far more economical in materials and labour than cut, carved and joined furniture; and it also allowed Thonet to introduce mechanized production methods and pare down surplus elements and ornament. As a result, in 1860 Thonet was able to sell his hugely popular *No. 14* chair for less than the price of a bottle of wine. The success of Gebrüder Thonet inspired a host of imitators, most notably Jakob & Josef Kohn of Vienna. Kohn's talented team of designers – including Gustav Siegel, Koloman Moser and Otto Wagner – celebrated the cap-

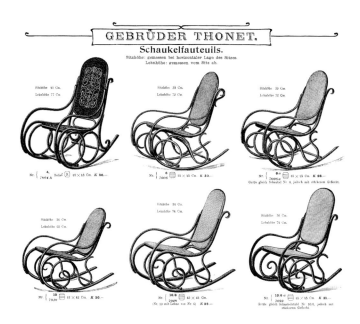

GEBRÜDER THONET.
Schaukelfauteuils.

abilities of bent wood within **Art Nouveau** and **Secessionist** furniture and interiors. From then on, however, bent wood and the **avant-garde** gradually
parted company. **Tubular metal** captured the imagination of Modernists,
and when wood was revisited in the 1930s and 1940s it was in the form of
moulded **plywood** and laminates. Nonetheless, the mechanized manufacture, economy of form and interchangeable components of Thonet's furniture had blazed the trail.

BIOMORPHISM

Carlo Graffi & Franco Campo, armchair, c. 1955

Unlike **Organic Design**, which is informed by nature and attempts to capture its abstract essence, Biomorphism copies and often distorts forms found in the natural world for purely decorative purposes. Biomorphism is not only characteristic of certain 20th-century styles, it can also be found in a number of much earlier period styles such as Baroque and Rococo. During the last quarter of the 19th century, significant advances in the understanding of the natural sciences were achieved and the natural world was seen by designers such as William Morris and Christopher Dresser as a lexicon of design. At the turn of the century, the general interest in botany was expressed through the biomorphic forms adopted by designers allied to **Art Nouveau**. These included swirling tendril-like motifs, elongated vegetal forms and a curious "melting" of naturalistic elements into one another. Once the Art Nouveau style had been super-seded by **Art Deco** and Modernism, Biomorphism did not re-emerge in design until the 1940s, when the highly biomorphic furniture of the Italian designer Carlo Mollino and his followers, sometimes referred to as Turinese Baroque, pushed the expressive potential of wood to the limit. In contrast, contemporary **avant-garde** designers in America, such as Charles and Ray Eames, were developing a vocabulary of design that was inherently organic. The forms of their products, such as the *LCW* chair of 1945, were informed by a sound understanding of humanizing factors including **ergonomics**. Designs such as these were extremely influential and led many mainstream designers to adopt biomorphic forms, especially asymmetrical kidney shapes. Indeed, it is these frequently **Kitsch** biomorphic shapes that are most often generally associated with the look of the 1950s. In the 1990s, Organic Design re-emerged, together with its stylistic spin-off, biomorphism. This was particularly evident in automotive design, where the trend was towards both progressive organic forms and retro-styled biomorphic forms, redolent of the 1950s.

BORAX

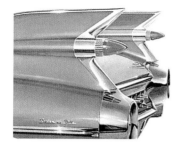

The tail fins of a 1959 Cadillac

Borax is a derogative term that refers to the American practice during the 1930s, '40s and '50s of adding surface details to products in an attempt to enhance their consumer appeal rather than their function. The term was derived from the famous Borax soap company and its well-known promotional strategy of give-away special offers. The Borax aesthetic had much in common with **Art Deco** styling and 1930s **streamlining**, in that it was highly expressive and frequently ostentatious. Typically relying on the liberal use of gleaming **chromium** detailing, Borax was extremely popular, but was also the very antithesis of **Good Design**. In 1948 it was the subject of a damning critique by Edgar Kaufmann in *Architectural Review*, entitled "Borax, or the chromium-plated calf". Common to cheap furniture and other domestic products, during the 1950s Borax found its most extreme expression in automotive styling and in particular the exaggerated tail fins on cars such as Harley Earl's 1959 *Eldorado* and *Fleetwood* Cadillacs. In Britain, the term Borax was also used during the post-war years to refer to extravagant streamlining and over-embellished surface treatments, such as those found on juke boxes. By the late-1950s, however, consumers in both the USA and Britain had become more design-literate and the surface glamour of Borax began to tarnish.

Pontiac *Firebird* concept car, c. 1959

BRANDING

Branded doll from
Sunny Jim flour

Pages from a
Cadbury's booklet
showing branded
gifts available with
Bournville Cocoa
coupons, 1935

Branding is the process through which meaning and value are added to products. At its simplest, a brand is a guarantee of authenticity and replicability, a badge of trustworthiness and a promise of performance. Thus, a brand exists as a collection of notions in the consumer's mind. Branding, however, can actually affect our perception of a product's physical characteristics and thus positively colour our experience of using the product. To this extent, branding is used widely by manufacturers as a cost-effective means of adding value to their products. On average, branding is responsible for over 80 % of a product's added value, yet accounts for only approximately 20 % of its cost. Manufacturers establish brand identity by various means, including naming, **packaging**, advertising and marketing. The idea of "brand personality" is also becoming an ever more important factor in the marketplace, as manufacturers attempt to differentiate their products from those of their competitors. Branding issues are thus increasingly a consideration

CHOCOLATE GIFTS

CADBURY'S
DAIRY MILK
CHOCOLATE

Gift No. 700 — ½ lb.
Cadbury's Milk Choco-
late, 2 oz. Bournville
Fruit and Nut Choco-
late, 2 oz. Milk, Fruit
and Nut Chocolate, 2
oz. Bournville Choco-
late.   15 Coupons.

Gift No. 701.— ½ lb.
Drum Cadbury's
Chocolate Table Bis-
cuts.   14 Coupons.

Gift No. 702.—Selec-
tion of Cadbury's 2d.
Chocolate Varieties.
          15 coupons.

Gift No. 703.—Large
Cocoa Jug, Whisk and
Measure.
          35 Coupons.

CHOCOLATE GIFTS

Gift No. 704.—Child's
Money Box containing
an assortment of Cad-
bury's Chocolates.
          13 coupons.

Gift No. 705.—Child's
Mug containing Cad-
bury's Milk Chocolate
Drops.   14 coupons.

Gift No. 706.—Small
Selection Box of Cad-
bury's Chocolates.
          15 coupons.

Gift No. 707.—Large
Selection Box of Cad-
bury's Chocolates.
(Two layers.)
          28 coupons.

How to obtain your gift.
SEE PAGE 5.

McDonald's restaurant at Des Plaines, Illinois, 1955 – the "golden arches" not only created a powerful brand image but came to symbolise post-war American lifestyle as well

for industrial designers working within the framework of an established brand identity, or required to incorporate brand names or logos in their overall design schemes. The importance of the relationship between **corporate identity** and branding is illuminated by the success of IBM, General Electric and Ford. These companies rank among the top five brands worldwide, a position they have achieved not least by investing enormous resources into integrated corporate design programmes that encompass brand strategies. The implementation of a house style for both product and packaging is a key to the establishment of brand identity. Thus the functionalist aesthetic of Braun products and the high-tech vocabulary of Bang & Olufsen audio-visual equipment make them instantly recognizable. Brand logos, too, speak a visual, trans-cultural language in which McDonald's "golden arches" and Nike's "swoosh" mean the same to consumers whether in Germany or in Thailand. Although in recent years it seemed that branded products were going to lose ground to cheaper no-name or own-brand products, the opposite has occurred, with brand identity carrying more weight than ever in today's highly competitive global marketplace. An outstanding example is Coca-Cola, ranked the world's most powerful brand according to a survey conducted in 2005, with a brand value of $67.5 billion (Pepsi is estimated to be worth only $12.3 billion). Where a branding pro-

Symbol of Friendship

gramme is successful, it should produce a differential and sustainable advantage over competitive products or services. Today, product differentiation through branding is especially critical in sectors where there is increasingly little to distinguish the performance and/or technological advantages of one product over another. Beyond price, the decision leading to the purchase of a particular product is increasingly governed by the consumer's perception of and identification with the brand.

CARBON FIBRE

Mike Burrows, *Mono* superbike, 1992

Carbon fibre is an advanced composite material in which a reinforcing element of woven graphite fibres is embedded in an epoxy matrix. The material is highly versatile and has two outstanding properties, strength and lightness, which makes it especially suitable for high-performance products that require minimum weight with high tensile resiliency. Carbon fibres have extremely high elastic modulus values (up to five times that of steel) and so make excellent reinforcement. Usually loosely woven into a type of cloth, the fibres are laid in the matrix according to the strength requirements of the design – areas where the fibres are most closely woven will be those of greatest stress. While carbon fibre is still a relatively new material, one of its most celebrated applications was in Mike Burrows' *Mono* superbike (1992) which was used by the British cyclist Chris Boardman to win a gold medal at the 1992 Barcelona Olympic Games. Carbon fibre is employed in state-of-the-art sports equipment, from golf clubs to kayaks, the aerospace industry and racing car components, all of which are fields of design where weight considerably affects performance. Carbon fibre has also been used experimentally in furniture, as in Alberto Meda's *Light Light* chair (1987). Constructed of a moulded carbon fibre skin surrounding a Nomex honeycomb core, this chair is remarkable for its strength yet extreme lightness, weighing only about 1 kg. Although the high cost of carbon fibre precludes its widespread use in mainstream consumer products, one of the most successful recent applications of the material has been in the serial production of ski helmets, with most manufacturers now using carbon fibre for their top-of-the-range models.

Carbon Racing 2.0 ski helmet for Carrera, 1999

CERAMICS

Josiah Wedgwood,
*The Apotheosis of
Homer vase, c. 1786*

Ceramic materials are derived from naturally-occurring inorganic materials such as clay minerals and quartz sand. Through production processes that have been refined over centuries, ceramics have been rendered into a wide variety of products including china tableware, bricks, tiles, industrial abrasives, refractory linings and even cement. The inherent malleability of clay makes ceramics ideally suited to moulding processes and, thereby, mass production. Ceramics may be said to represent one of the very first processed materials used in the service of design, clay having been fashioned into ceramic pots and vessels since the earliest times. In Ancient Rome, oil lamps were replicated using decorated plaster moulds – an early example of serial manufacture. It was not until the mid-18th century, however, that the English potter Josiah Wedgwood became the first to truly industrialize the manufacture of ceramic wares. Due to their inherent resistance to chemical attack, ceramics can also be used for **packaging**, a practice especially widespread in the days before **plastics**. The last 20 years have seen the development of a new breed of high-tech engineering ceramics, with numerous industrial applications ranging from combustion engine

Ceramic dispensing
pots, England, 19th
century

Seymour Powell, *Zero* knives (internal study project), 1998 – using zirconia ceramics

components to oxygen sensors. These highly sophisticated materials are completely different from traditional ceramics in that they include in their composition metallic powders such as alumina, titania, yttria and zirconia. This lends them significantly different properties, most notably exceptional wear and corrosion resistance, high hardness and strength, and makes them suitable for – among many other things – cutting blades. Today, material scientists are pioneering other advanced ceramics that can be injection-moulded and finished to remarkably accurate tolerances. "Bio ceramics" have also been developed for various medical implants including hip replacements – the material's bio-inert properties, strength and toughness making it ideal for such applications. Ceramics have not only played an important role historically in the evolution of industrial design, but are considered by many to be the engineering materials of the future.

CHROMIUM

Chromium is a hard metallic element that can be polished to produce a gleaming reflective surface. It is often used as an alloy to strengthen other metals, especially steel, and to increase their resistance to oxidation and corrosion. While a relatively abundant element, chromium always occurs as a compound, most commonly as chromite. Although the element was first discovered in 1797 by the French chemist Louis-Nicolas Vauquelin, it was not until the First World War that it found a useful application as a coating material for shell casings. In 1925 it became widely available and was subsequently used decoratively for **Art Deco** furnishings and as a corrosion-resistant coating for Modernist **tubular metal** furniture. During the 1930s, American designers made extensive use of chromium plating, as the brilliance of its reflectivity accentuated the seductive streamlined forms of their product designs. The material had its true heyday in the 1950s, however, when each year's new car models were laden with ever more chromium-plated elements, which were intended to exude a sense of luxury.

COLOUR IN DESIGN

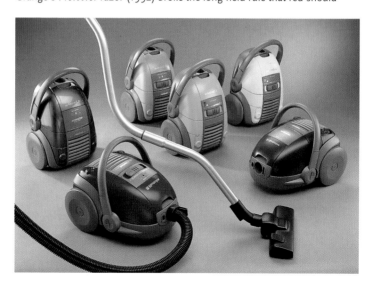

Kenneth Grange, *Protector* razor for Wilkinson Sword, 1992

The colour of a product is very often determined not by the designer but by their client, who sometimes employs an independent colour consultant to predict future trends in preference. This type of fashion-driven colour selection, however, belies the importance of colour in product design. Colour can radically alter the visual perception of a product and can dramatically highlight its form – the classic example being the red used for Ferrari automobiles. Colour can also be used to make a product more user-friendly – the limited use of colour in Braun alarm clocks, for example, highlights the product's various functions. Colour can furthermore be used to visually update an existing product so as to buy time for the manufacturer to develop its successor. While there are many conventions relating to the use of colour, a number of these have been famously overthrown with spectacular results. Jonathan Ive's *iMac* computer (1998), for example, brilliantly contradicted the notion that all computers must be grey, while Kenneth Grange's *Protector* razor (1992) broke the long-held rule that red should

Electrolux *Oxygen* vacuum cleaner in assorted colours, 1999

Alessandro Mendini,
Anna G. corkscrews
for Alessi, 1994

never be used for shaving products because of the colour's association
with blood. Designers and manufacturers also have to be mindful of different cultural associations with colour. White, for example, is recognized as
a symbol of purity in Western cultures yet is associated with mourning in
China. There are also many cultural variations in colour preference – south-
ern Europeans tend to prefer red or white cars, while northern Europeans
tend to prefer black or silver. Colour is an important aspect of industrial
design as it can have strong psychological and physiological effects on product users. Colour selection, therefore, should be treated as an integral part
of the design process rather than as an afterthought motivated by the whims
of fashion.

COMPASSO D'ORO

FOUNDED 1954
MILAN, ITALY

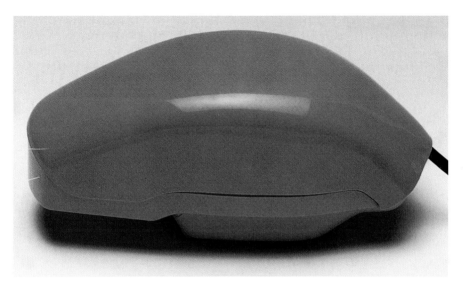

**Marco Zanuso &
Richard Sapper,**
Grillo telephone for
Siemens, 1965

The Compasso d'Oro awards were founded by the La Rinascente department store owner, Aldo Borletti, in 1954. Borletti stated that the awards were "to encourage industrialists and craftsmen to raise their production standards both from a technological and aesthetic standpoint". Initially, the Compasso d'Oro prizes were only awarded for the design of objects retailed and distributed by La Rinascente. From 1959, the ADI (Associazione per Il Disegno Industriale) helped in the running of the awards and, in 1967, completely took over their administration. The ADI widened the range and types of products eligible for the awards and thus ensured international recognition of the Compasso d'Oro's status. Notable winners have included Marcello Nizzoli for the *Lettera 22* typewriter for Olivetti (won in 1954) and the *Mirella* sewing machine for Necchi (1957), Marco Zanuso & Richard Sapper for the *Doney 14* television for Brionvega (1962) and *Grillo* telephone for Siemens (1967), Achille & Pier Giacomo Castiglioni for their vacuum cleaner for R. E. M. (1957) and Mario Bellini for the *Totem* record player/radio for Brionvega (1979).

COMPUTER-AIDED DESIGN/ -MANUFACTURE (CAD/CAM)

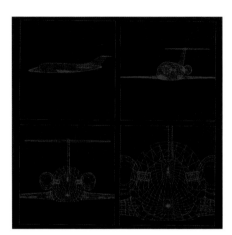

Computer-Aided Design (CAD) was first developed at the renowned Massachusetts Institute of Technology in the 1950s. During the early days of computers, however, CAD software was relatively primitive and was rarely used outside the aerospace and automotive industries. As hardware became increasingly more powerful in terms of both memory and processing speed, and at the same time less expensive, so CAD began to gain a foothold in the design community. Today CAD is a powerful and essential tool with which designers can prepare drawings and translate them into three-dimensional

IBM 5080 graphics system, which can pan, zoom and rotate two-dimensional and three-dimensional models, late 1990s

models (either in solid form or made up of structural lines) that can be rotated, scaled, zoomed, panned or cross-sectioned. The information derived from CAD programmes can then be translated by Computer-Aided Manufacture (CAM) software into useable data that assists in the control of the machines (such as lathes and cutting tools) and robots used in the production process. Primary amongst the many benefits of employing a CAD/ CAM combination are thus greater engineering precision and increased productivity. CAD/CAM programmes are not only invaluable in ensuring the **standardization** of components but also permit greater flexibility in the manufacturing process, allowing for lower-volume or irregular, batch-type production. Significantly, CAD/CAM can also dramatically reduce the time-lapse from initial concept to working prototype, thereby making the design process more efficient and enabling manufacturers to get new products to the marketplace even quicker. The use of computers has brought about a revolution in the design industry and has led directly to the development of safer and better performing products.

CONSTRUCTIVISM

Nikolai Suetin, writing set for the State Porcelain Factory in Petrograd, 1923

Wassily Kandinsky, coffee cup and saucer for the State Porcelain Factory in Petrograd, 1921

The term Constructivism refers to a movement primarily in Russian art, design and architecture. Prior to the First World War, the Russian **avant-garde**, like their European counterparts, were inspired by Cubism and **Futurism**. After the 1917 revolution, however, the Russian avant-garde sought new forms of expression that related to the Soviet desire to supplant the capitalist system with more democratic schemes for the production and distribution of goods. To this end, artists such as Vladimir Tatlin, Kasimir Malevich, Alexander Rodchenko, Wassily Kandinsky, Naum Gabo, Antoine Pevsner and El Lissitzky began promoting an aesthetic and approach to design that was allied to industrial production. The publication of two manifestos in 1920, *The Programme of the Group of Constructivists* by Alexei Gan, Varvara Stepanova and Rodchenko and *A Realistic Manifesto* by Pevsner and Gabo, heralded the emergence of Constructivism. The Constructivists believed that the applied arts could bring about a new social order and so began creating utilitarian "production art" and architecture. The political and economic instability that followed the revolution, however, meant that few large-scale projects were undertaken and the Constructivists' output was mainly confined to the fields of exhibition design, ceramics and graphics. Constructivist ceramics were often decorated with Suprematist motifs – geometric forms set against plain white backgrounds – which produced a strong sense of dynamism and modernity.

CORPORATE IDENTITY

Raymond Loewy,
redesigned bottle
and drinks dispenser
for Coca-Cola,
c. 1948

Corporate identity design, which is strongly related to **packaging** design, is a means by which companies and/ or brands can give their products or services a visually unified character that will differentiate them from others in the marketplace. Central to corporate identity is the company logo, which is normally used on all corporate projections from stationery to advertising. Some mainly design-led companies and brands, such as Braun, adopt a holistic approach to corporate identity, implementing a rigorously-managed design regime which impacts not only on the nature of their products but on the design of their offices and factories as well. Peter Behrens was the first designer to put such a programme into action when he became the artistic adviser to AEG in 1907. He applied an integrated language of design not just to the company's products and graphics, but to housing for its workers and even one of its factories – all of which was instrumental in forging AEG's easily recognizable identity. In view of the progressive globalization of today's markets, commercial organizations are increasingly embracing the universal language of corporate identity design in an effort to compete more effectively.

Peter Behrens, logos
for AEG, 1908–1914

Raymond Loewy
Associates, logos
for Shell, 1967, and
BP, 1938; Landor
Associates, Logos
for Alitalia, 1969,
and Spar, 1970

←Selection of
corporate logos
designed by
Raymond Loewy
Associates

ALPHA CREDIT BANK

ELECTRICITY AUTHORITY OF CYPRUS

CRAFT REVIVAL

The origins of the Craft Revival can be traced to the mid-19th century when design reformers such as John Ruskin and William Morris urged for the preservation and revitalization of traditional crafts in the wake of unprecedented industrialization in Britain. The success of Morris & Co., which produced and retailed handcrafted vernacular-style products, inspired the following generation of designers aligned to the **Arts & Crafts Movement**, such as Charles Voysey, Charles R. Ashbee and A. H. Mackmurdo. During the 1880s, some members of the movement founded guilds, such as the Art Worker's Guild, the Century Guild and the Guild of Handicraft. Later designers affiliated with the movement based in the Cotswolds, such as Ernest Gimson, Sidney and Edward Barnsley and Gordon Russell, advocated a more austere form of vernacularism based on functional appropriateness. Arts & Crafts designers in America, such as Gustav Stickley, Elbert H. Hubbard and Frank Lloyd Wright were also instigating a return to vernacularism in design and traditional craftsmanship through their promotion of the Mission style. From the mid-20th century, as industrial manufacturing processes offered ever greater possibilities, design and production became increasingly divorced from one another and craft skills went into decline. To reverse this

John Makepeace,
Millenium 3 chair,
1988

trend, John Makepeace and Wendell Castle, two of the most important protagonists of the Craft Revival in the late 20th century, have preserved craft skills through their work as designer-makers and through their schools for craftsmen in wood. During the 1980s, the Craft Revival was stylistically accomplished by **Post-Modernism**, and designers such as Fred Baier combined technical virtuosity with bizarre forms to create objects that were the very antithesis of the "good citizen's furniture" that had been espoused by Morris and Ruskin.

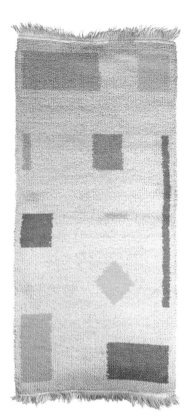

Bart van der Leck,
carpet for Metz &
Co., 1918–1919

DE STIJL

FOUNDED 1917
NETHERLANDS

In October 1917, a small group of Dutch architects, designers and artists established an art journal entitled *De Stijl*. Led by Theo van Doesburg, the group initially included Piet Mondrian, Bart Anthony van der Leck, Vilmos Huszár, Jacobus Johannes Pieter Oud, Robert van't Hoff, Jan Wils and Georges Vantongerloo. The magazine became a forum for art and design debates and eventually the focus of a larger and wider ranging group of intellectuals. This loosely organized movement shared a common objective, that of absolute abstraction. The journal not only featured the latest developments in **avant-garde** Dutch art and design but also the work of the Russian Constructivists, the Dadaists and the Italian Futurists. The publication called for a purification of art and design through the adoption of a universal language of abstracted Cubism or, as Piet Mondrian described it, Neo-Plasticism. De Stijl members believed that the search for honesty and beauty would ultimately bring harmony and enlightenment to humanity. Theo van Doesburg, who was editor-in-chief of the magazine, tirelessly promoted the De Stijl message on his numerous trips to Belgium, France, Italy and Germany. In 1921, he established contacts with staff at the Staatliches **Bauhaus** in Weimar, and a year later gave a De Stijl course of lectures in Weimar. Theo van Doesburg also developed links with Constructivists, such as El Lissitzky and László Moholy-Nagy. The De Stijl movement not only influenced developments in the fine arts, its members also designed extremely influential furniture, interiors, textiles, graphics and architecture. Gerrit Rietveld's revolutionary *Red/Blue* chair of 1918–1923, which in its design encapsulated the philosophy of the De Stijl Movement, was exhibited at the Staatliche Bauhaus in 1923 and inspired Marcel Breuer's later **tubular metal** *B3 Wassily* chair of 1925–1927. Like Rietveld's *Red/Blue* chair, De Stijl architecture and interior designs were characterized by the use of strong geometric forms and coloured block-like elements that delineated space. Partitions were used to divide internal areas, while utilitarian furnishings were kept to an absolute minimum. The strong lines incorporated in these interiors produced a dynamism, while a sense of lightness was achieved through the purging of ornament. This essentialist approach to design was highly influential to the development of the **Modern Movement**, as was De Stijl's use of geometric formalism. Although the De Stijl group was never formally organized, its output was highly distinctive and shared a common visual language – that of geometric abstraction. The application of this new vocabulary of form and colour blurred the traditional distinctions between the fine and decorative arts, but sadly the group's intention of bringing a greater universality to the arts was never fully realized. The De Stijl movement's vision of Utopia was inspired by the vitality of the modern city, while its utilitarian approach to the design of objects for use was influenced by Dutch Puritanism. Though sharing many of the ideas propounded by Russian **Constructivism**, such as spatial dynamism, De Stijl is

Gerrit Rietveld,
isometric drawing
of the interior of the
Rietveld-Schroeder
House in Utrecht,
1927

generally acknowledged as the first modern design movement, because it heralded a new aesthetic purity. The *De Stijl* magazine was published until Theo van Doesburg's death in 1931, after which the movement gradually lost its focus and was unable to maintain its former momentum.

DECONSTRUCTIVISM

Daniel Weil, *Radio in a Bag* for Parenthesis, 1981–1983

Deconstruction is a method of analysis primarily associated with literary criticism that was first postulated in the 1960s by the French philosopher Jacques Derrida. Through his writings, he argued that by analysing or "deconstructing" the logic of Western metaphysics, its underlying biases could be uncovered. Deconstruction was also used to demonstrate that because a creative work is subject to different interpretations, its content is ultimately ambiguous, which in turn undermines its logic. By deconstructing the formal language of the **Modern Movement**, its multiplicity of meanings and biases were revealed, which resulted in the questioning of its philosophical foundations. During the 1970s, Derrida's ideas were translated and transformed into a style of architecture and design – Deconstructivism. The style is allied to **Post-Modernism**, as it counters the traditional premises of Modernism. However, unlike Post-Modernism, it rejects historicism and ornamentation. Likewise, Deconstructivism often alludes to the deconstruction of meaning, whereas Post-Modernism playfully subverts meaning and double-codes it. Stylistically if not philosophically similar to Russian **Constructivism** of the 1920s, Deconstructivism also adopted fragmented and expressive forms. Its most notable practitioners in architecture and interior design are Frank O. Gehry, Coop Himmelb(l)au (founded 1968), Zaha Hadid, Peter Eisenman and Bernard Tschumi. Being an essentially anti-rational style, Deconstructivism is linked to **Anti-Design** and has had little impact on product design, apart from a few examples such as Daniel Weil's *Radio in a Bag* (1981–1983), which by revealing its constituent parts countered traditional forms and deconstructed conventional design logic.

DESIGN FOR CHILDREN

Random Techno-
logies, *Kid's Phone*,
1998 (prototype)

Products for children are designed within a completely different set of parameters than those for adults, and fall into two main categories – equipment and toys.

The equipment category embraces everything from feeding cups to pushchairs (strollers) and is primarily governed by function, although changing social trends also play a part. Thus the prams or "baby carriages" which date back to the 18th century and were the norm in Western society until the 1960s have now given way to pushchairs such as the lightweight folding Maclaren baby buggy, which when introduced in 1967 quite literally transformed the transportation of infants. Generally speaking, well-designed children's equipment will be ergonomically resolved for ease of handling, strongly constructed, characterized by smoothed surfaces for hygiene and the prevention of injury, and brightly coloured so as to attract the child's attention. All of these features are found in the design of the *Anyway* cup. A prototypical design that also fulfilled these criteria was the *Kid's Phone* produced by Random Technologies. This product featured a simple layout with a "home" button that could be used by a child to call home even if they forgot their telephone number. The children's toy category is governed by similar criteria to equipment, with the most successful designs, such as Lego and Meccano, providing children of all ages with hours of stimulating creative play. The majority of toys, however, are poorly designed, being driven more by marketing strategies and profit margins than any real desire for quality. Among the worst examples of this type of consumerist design are the "free" give-away toys that are common to fast-food restaurants. The play content of these toys is more often than not as short-lived as the meal that accompanies them. As future consumers, this is surely not the way to instil in children the importance of **Good Design** and of responsible consumption.

Anyway cup for V&A
Marketing, c. 1999

DESIGN FOR DISABILITY

A&E Design, *Handy* extension handles for Etac, 1977

Design for disability falls into the category of "virtuous design", but could equally be called "design for ability" because it helps to empower users. The history of this design discipline can be traced to the development of sedan chairs and the later invalid carriages of the 18th and 19th centuries. It was not until the 1950s, however, that leading designers became involved in the design of products for the disabled – one of the earliest examples being an amputee's hook (c. 1950) designed by Henry Dreyfuss in collaboration with the Army Prosthetics Research Laboratory and the Sierra Engineering Company. This innovative device was designed so that with a slight flexing of the shoulder muscles the hook could be opened and closed, thus enabling the user to handle relatively small objects including coins and matches. Until the 1960s, equipment for the disabled was designed from a medical perspective and little if any thought was given to their aesthetic appearance. It was around this time, however, that an international disability symbol was devised and public environments began to be adapted or designed for greater accessibility. In 1969 *Design* magazine devoted a whole issue to the subject of design for disability, and two years later Victor Papanek's highly influential *Design for a Real World* was published. Highlighting the need for better design solutions, Papanek wrote: "Cerebral palsy, poliomyelitis, myasthenia gravis, Mongoloid cretinism, and many other crippling diseases and accidents affect one-tenth of the American public and their families (20 million people) and approximately 400 million people around the world. Yet the design of prosthetic devices, wheelchairs, and other invalid gear is by and large still on a Stone Age level." During the 1970s, the greatest advances in the design of enabling products for handicapped people were made in Sweden, most notably by A&E Design and Ergonomi Design Gruppen. The latter designed numerous products including the well-known *Eat and Drink* combination cutlery, drinking vessels and plates (1980) for RSFU Rehab. The design excellence of these products led one British theorist,

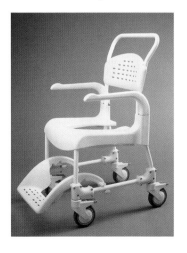

A&E Design, *Clean* shower and toilet chair, 1999

David Farrage of
Smart Design, *Good
Grip* scrub brushes
for OXO, 1997

↗**Smart Design**,
Good Grip vegetable
peeler for OXO,
1990s

James Woudhuysen, to ask, in the "Svensk Form" exhibition catalogue (1981), whether it was a handicap not to be handicapped in Sweden. Other life-enhancing products developed over the 1980s and 1990s included London Innovation Limited's *Neater Eater* device, which enabled people suffering from severe tremors to feed themselves, and Motivation's wheelchairs, developed predominantly for use in third world countries using locally available components. Over recent years, the Design for Ability organization based at Central St Martin's College of Art & Design in London, has conducted extensive market research into the needs of disabled people and made the findings available to the design community, resulting in better-performing and better-looking products such as Tangerine's *Activ* walking frame, which bears little relation to its predecessor – the scaffolding-like *Zimmer*. The *Good Grips* range of kitchen equipment, which includes numerous easy-to-use products from dustpans and brushes to potato mashers, was developed by Sam Farber in response to a paper written by Mary Reader for the *Journal of the Institute of Home Economics*, in which she called for the development of "transgenerational" kitchen tools. Having noted that most kitchen tools were "at best indifferent and at worst hostile", especially to those suffering from arthritis, Faber and his wife Betsey commissioned the New York-based consultancy, Smart Design, to design a new range of tools without losing "sight of the final user". The subsequent introduction in 1989 of the *Good Grips* collection of everyday domestic tools with soft rubber ergonomic handles signalled a completely new approach to design for disability – inclusive design for most members of society regardless of age or physical ability.

DESIGN FOR SAFETY

Chubb fire extinguisher *Model WS9*, 1979

⬎Highmask Manufacturing & Co., Anti-stab vest, 2000 – selected as a Millennium Product by Design Council

Protector Technology, *Tornado* respirator, 2000

The issue of safety is a relatively recent phenomenon within the history of industrial design. It first came to widespread public attention when the young lawyer and consumer advocate, Ralph Nader, wrote a damning critique of the American automobile industry, *Unsafe at any Speed: the Designed-In Dangers of the American Automobile* (1965), which focused in particular on the design flaws of the Chevrolet *Corvair* (1960). This unusual looking mid-engine car was a potential killer because of its tendency to roll over when cornering sharply. While the management of General Motors was aware of this defect, it cynically decided to put profit before safety and continued with production. At the time, it was estimated that General Motors spent about $700 on **styling** per car but only around 23 cents on safety features. Nader's landmark legal triumph over this automotive giant heralded not only the beginning of the product liability industry but also the widespread awareness of safety issues within both the design and manufacturing industries. Design for safety falls into two main categories – the development of products

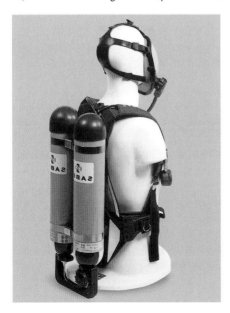

that are safer to use, and the design of safety equipment such as fire extinguishers, seat belts, airbags, smoke alarms, breathing apparatus etc. Some car companies such as Volvo are renowned for their remarkably long record of developing innovative safety "firsts", while others will only go as far as safety legislation compels them. The design of safer products has been assisted considerably, however, by the introduction of safety standards. These are effectively guidelines, drawn up by committees composed of representatives of relevant industries and then submitted to a process of public consultation. The resulting standards are in many cases incorporated into legislation governing product design and manufacture (e. g. the banning of certain furniture upholstering foams in Europe). In the sphere of toy manufacture, for example, toys complying with European Directives are allowed to bear the "CE" mark, enabling them to be imported and exported from one member state to another. Although such legislation is increasingly effective in improving product safety, designed products continue to cause injuries and fatalities. In some cases, increasing competitiveness leads design consultancies to just "give the client what they want", without any real in-depth consideration of potential safety issues.

DESIGN FOR SPORT

Sycamore Origination, *SpinGrip Outsole* football boot for Umbro, c. 1999 – selected as a Millennium Product by the Design Council

Sports equipment is one of the most interesting areas of design practice as it frequently involves pushing materials and technology to new heights of performance. In competition sports, how well a piece of equipment is designed can not merely make the difference between winning and losing, but can redefine the parameters of the sport itself. In recent years, for example, Atomic *Beta Race* skis, whose parabolic shape and highly innovative Beta titanium construction facilitate more precise and aggressive carving, have dominated World Cup skiing to such an extent that they have affected the design of race courses. Because sports equipment relies heavily on research and development, many companies have their own in-house design teams and only rarely commission an independent designer to produce new products for them. Sports equipment is often initially developed using state-of-the-art **Computer-Aided Design** (CAD) technology in accordance with the latest **ergonomics** data, and is then extensively field-tested by company-sponsored athletes so that the designs can be further honed. The knowledge gained from these trials is then incorporated into designs for mass production. The best-performing sports equipment, whether for competition or leisure use, is generally that which is designed to act like body prosthetics, which respond to every move that is made. Although the design of sports equipment is often evolutionary, it can also be revolutionary, as in the case of the *Windcheetah* recumbent high-performance vehicle (1992) designed by Mike Burrows, and the *Sea-Doo* personal watercraft invented by Bombardier in 1968. The manufacture and retail of sports equipment is now big busi-

Big Bertha metal drivers for Callaway Golf, 1991

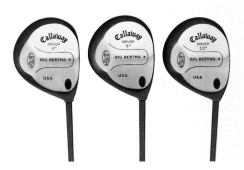

ness, but it is nonetheless subject to the vagaries of fashion. Sometimes a product that is heralded as a significant innovation performs only minimally better than its predecessors and is therefore of only limited benefit to the amateur user. It is human nature, however, to believe that a new design – whether a golf club or a pair of football boots – will dramatically improve one's game or performance, and perhaps this produces at least a placebo effect. Frequently, new lightweight yet robust materials find their first mass applications in the field of sports design, as with the introduction of **carbon fibre** in the construction of ski helmets. Over recent years, the design of sportswear and sports equipment has had an enormous influence on the mainstream fashion industry.

←**Continuum of Milan**, Atomic *Beta Race* skis, 1997

↙**Giugiaro Design**, in-line skate for Tecnica, 1999

↘*Bug* sports chronograph for Animal, 1999

DESIGN FOR THE THIRD WORLD

Motivation, *Mekong* wheelchair, 1993

Behind the concept of design for the Third World lies the goal of empowering developing nations to meet their own needs in ways which make economic and environmental sense. Culturally appropriate design can not only dramatically enhance the lives of those most in need, but – vitally, in the longer term – can also provide some of the key foundations upon which regional economies can be built. Examples of this type of design include the wheelchairs designed by Motivation for landmine victims, which are built from locally available components, the pedal-powered washing machines developed by the Industrial Design Laboratory of the University of Paraiba in Brazil, and the *Freeplay* self-powered radios and torches designed by Trevor Baylis, which are now manufactured in South Africa. Unfortunately, few Western designers have felt compelled to work within this extremely worthy area of design because it is generally regarded as financially unprofitable. The solution to this problem lies in education, as mooted by Victor Papanek in his seminal book, *Design for a Real World* (1971). Here he put forward the idea of Western designers travelling from one developing country to another, in order to train people from "the indigenous population of the country [in order] to create a group of designers firmly committed to their own cultural heritage, their own lifestyle, and their own needs."

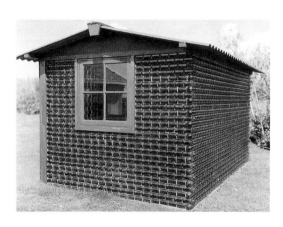

WOBO (WOrld BOttle) house study and prototype bottles commissioned by A. H. Heineken, early 1960s – an unrealized proposal for shelters constructed from specially designed beer bottles

Founder members
of the Deutscher
Werkbund

DEUTSCHER WERKBUND

FOUNDED 1907
MUNICH, GERMANY

In 1906, the III Deutsche Kunstgewerbeausstellung
(German Arts & Crafts Exhibition) held in Dresden revealed that the expressive **Jugendstil** style was being
overtaken by a more formal language of design that
emphasized function. Only those designs that were the
result of a positive collaboration between designers
associated with established workshops, such as the
Dresdener Werkstätten für Handwerkskunst were
shown. This work was more utilitarian than any previously exhibited in Dresden and reflected the realization
of designers, such as Richard Riemerschmid, that the
only way to produce large quantities of well-designed
and executed products that were also affordable was through the manufacturing industry. In promoting this new direction, the exhibition highlighted
a new aesthetic and social imperative in design and acted as a catalyst for
the formation of the Deutscher Werkbund. Founded in October 1907, the
Deutscher Werkbund attempted from its outset to reconcile artistic endeavour with industrial mass-production. Thus, its founding body was made up
of a dozen designers, including Riemerschmid, Bruno Paul, Peter Behrens
and Josef Maria Olbrich, and a dozen established manufacturers, including
Peter Bruckmann & Söhne and Poeschel & Trepte, as well as design workshops, such as the **Wiener Werkstätte** and the Munich-based Vereinigte
Werkstätten für Kunst im Handwerk. Peter Bruckmann was appointed the
association's first president, and within a year its membership had risen to
around five hundred. From 1912, the Werkbund began publishing its own
yearbooks, which included articles with illustrations on its members' designs, such as factories by Walter Gropius and Peter Behrens and cars by
Ernst Naumann. The yearbooks also listed members' addresses and areas
of specialization, in an attempt to promote collaboration between art and
industry. In 1914, the Werkbund organized a landmark exhibition in Cologne,
entitled "Deutsche Werkbund-Ausstellung", which included Walter Gropius'
steel and glass model factory, Bruno Taut's Glass Pavilion and Henry van
de Velde's Werkbund Theatre. A year later, the Werkbund's membership had
swollen to almost two thousand. The increasing divergence between crafts-

→ **Fritz Hellmut Ehmke**, poster for the Deutsche Werkbund Exhibition in Cologne, 1914

manship and industrial production, however, continued to fuel a debate within the Werkbund, with some members such as Hermann Muthesius and Naumann arguing for standardization, while others such as van de Velde, Gropius and Taut argued for individualism. This conflict, known as the "Werkbundstreit" almost led to the disbanding of the association. The widespread need for consumer products after the devastation of the First World War, however, led Gropius to accept the necessity of standardization and industrial production, although other members such as Hans Poelzig continued to resist change. From 1921 to 1926, Riemerschmid was president of the Deutscher Werkbund and during his tenure the Functionalists' approach to design was advanced. In 1924, the Werkbund published *Form ohne Ornament* (*Form without Ornament*), which presented industrially produced designs and expounded on the virtues of plain undecorated surfaces and ultimately, **Functionalism**. In 1927, the Werkbund staged a unique exhibition in Stuttgart, entitled "Die Wohnung" (The Dwelling), which was organized by Ludwig Mies van der Rohe. The focus of the exhibition was a housing estate project, the "Weissenhofsiedlung", for which the most progressive architects throughout Europe were invited to design buildings. The interiors of these specially commissioned houses were furnished with modern **tubular metal** furniture designed by Mies van der Rohe, Mart Stam, Marcel Breuer and Le Corbusier among others. Widely publicized, this exhibition led to a greater acceptance of Modernism. Although the Werkbund was eventually disbanded in 1934, it was re-established in 1947 but was by then a spent force. The Deutscher Werkbund bridged Jugendstil and the **Modern Movement** and, through its activities, had an enormous impact on the evolution of German **industrial design**.

ENVIRONMENTAL DESIGN

Neo Ball fluorescent light bulb developed by Toshiba, 1998 – has six times the life of an ordinary bulb and uses a quarter of the energy

Environmental design is primarily concerned with minimizing waste and reducing the throughput of energy and materials in our society to sustainable levels. It was most famously pioneered by Richard Buckminster Fuller, who in the 1920s promoted a "design science" that was based on the concept of "providing the most with the least". It was he who, in the 1950s, coined the term "Spaceship Earth", which led people to think of the planet in a more holistic way. Other writers and theorists who have contributed to a greater understanding of environmental design include Vance Packard, whose book *The Waste Makers* (1961) was particularly damning of the practice of **planned obsolescence,** and Victor Papanek, author of *Design for a Real World* (1971), who related ecological awareness to the design process and urged for radical design solutions that were mindful of the environment. Views such as these were given greater currency in the early 1970s, when the oil crisis increased concern about the finite aspect of the world's natural resources. By the 1980s, several man-made environmental disasters, plus the growing realization that industrialization was contributing to global warming, had underlined the urgent need for environmental design. Environmental design – also known as "green design" – takes into consideration a product's whole life-cycle: the extraction of raw materials and the ecological impact of their processing; the energy consumed in the manufacturing process, together with any negative by-products; the energy required for and the impact of the distribution system; the length of a product's service life; component recovery and the efficiency of recyclability; and the ultimate effects of disposal on the environment through, for instance, landfill or incineration. Although

Pencil made of a recycled vending cup by Remarkable Pencil Limited, 1998

MADE FROM 1 RECYCLED VENDING CUP

Ecco Design,
SolarBlind (proto-
type), 1993 – solar-
powered light-
emitting blind

recycling can reduce energy consumption, it does not minimize it and
in some ways can be seen to actually perpetuate the throwaway culture.
Increased product durability, on the other hand, minimizes waste and
energy consumption – by doubling the useful life of a product, its environmental impact can be halved.

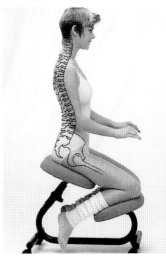

ERGONOMICS

Zdenek Kovar, ergonomic design for scissors, 1952

Peter Opsvik, *Balans Variable* chair for Stokke, 1979

Ergonomics, or "human factors" as it is more commonly known in the United States, is the systematic study of the characteristics of human users and their relationship with products, systems and environments. Closely related to **anthropometrics** (the systematic collection and correlation of human body measurements), ergonomics is concerned with anatomical, physiological and psychological factors in conjunction with human behaviour, capabilities and limitations. Through the scientific application of this data, ergonomics permits the design of better-performing, safer and more user-friendly solutions that are also easier to maintain and understand. In the workplace, therefore, ergonomics leads to greater efficiency and productivity. Because an ergonomic product is designed to work in harmony with the human body, it is also very often more comfortable to use, be it a pair of kitchen scissors or a chair. In terms of office seat furniture, where the provision of continuous flexible support is essential for healthful sitting, it is true to say that the majority of the ergonomic principles which now inform the design of chairs are based on human weaknesses, rather than on strengths. The remarkable success of Emilio Ambasz's *Vertebra* chair (1977), which was the first office chair to respond automatically to the body's movement, was almost entirely due to the fact that its design was based on ergonomic principles. Today's health and safety legislation, especially that governing the work environment, has ensured that ergonomic factors are increasingly taken into account by designers and manufacturers. As the International Centre of Ergonomics states: "Whether at work, on the road or in the home, ergonomics provides solutions that maximize convenience and effectiveness whilst minimizing the risk of accidents and injuries." The emergence of **Computer-Aided Design** (CAD) has further helped facilitate the application of ergonomic data to the design of products, systems and environments that are more functionally unified with the people who use them.

ESSENTIALISM

Ross Lovegrove,
Solar Bud eco-light
for Luceplan,
1996–1997

Essentialism is an approach to design concerned with
the logical arrangement of only those elements which
are absolutely necessary for the accomplishment of
a particular purpose. To this extent, essentialism is
based on the Modern concept of getting the most from the least and is
quite closely linked to **environmental design**. The origins of essentialism
can be traced to the Dymaxion (dynamic + maximum efficiency) design
science pioneered by Richard Buckminster Fuller in the 1920s, and Fuller's
subsequent attempts to bring about innovative design solutions using a
minimum of energy and materials. An essentialist approach to design frequently relies on a technologically-driven logic of construction and thus
has much in common with functionalist and rationalist design traditions.
Essentialism has characterized the work of many of the 20th century's leading industrial designers, yet the formal vocabulary of their designs has often
varied considerably. Seen as an evolution of Modernism, essentialism can
assume either geometric or organic form. There is no one defining style –
a design by Dieter Rams, for example, does not have the same aesthetic
qualities as a design by Charles Eames, yet both can be deemed Modern

Ross Lovegrove,
Detail of *Oasis* chair
for Driade, 1997

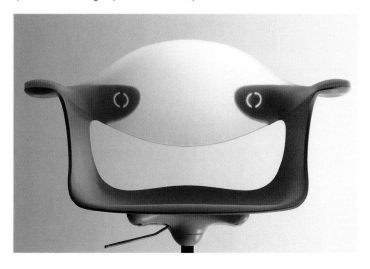

and utterly essentialist. Contemporary industrial designers such as Jasper Morrison and Konstanin Grcic take an almost utilitarian approach to design in order to create essentialist products that have an intense aesthetic purity. Other contemporary designers such as Harri Koskinen look to inherently essentialist vernacular design paradigms in order to reinterpret them in a modern idiom. Essentialism is increasingly partnering **Organic Design** and a new naturalism of form, as exemplified by the work of Ross Lovegrove. Commenting on the confusion that often exists between the pared-down formal vocabulary of essentialism, which is also known as "dematerialism", and minimalist **styling**, Lovegrove states: "I'm suspicious of minimalism because it doesn't really exist in nature ... I'm suspicious of it because I think life is not minimalist, generally it is quite complicated and detailed. Dematerialism – or essentialism – is another thing and relates more to the physicality of artefacts. Dematerialism means placing less emphasis on weight, density and thickness. It's the idea that things could be built in the future perhaps more organically, less constructed physically, growing rather than constructed ... Dematerialism is an absolute objective." While essentialism requires a great deal of understanding of structure, the nature of materials and industrial techniques, it is clearly the most appropriate approach to design for the 21st century.

Testing of *Model T*
starting device, 1914

FORDISM

Fordism is a term used to describe mass production – a method of manufacture that has dominated the economies of most developed countries since the early 20th century. Named after Henry Ford, who pioneered an assembly-line system of production for his *Model T* car, Fordism revolutionized not only the structure of the work process but also the way in which products were conceived and designed. As a result of the overwhelming demand in North America for the *Model T*, which was launched in 1908, Ford turned to the problem of producing the car in large volumes and at a low unit cost. His solution of a moving assembly line, which involved the optimal arrangement of machines, equipment and workers for the continuous flow of workpieces, was inspired by the meat-packing industry in Cincinnati and Chicago. Here, meat was processed industrially on a very large scale with animal carcasses being moved past workers at a steady pace via a system of electrically-powered overhead trolleys. Stationary workers concentrated on one task, performing it at a pace dictated by the mechanized line, minimizing unnecessary movement and greatly increasing productivity. Drawing upon his observations of these techniques and the theories of Frederick Winslow Taylor – whose seminal book, *The Principles of Scientific Management* (1911), outlined the precepts of what became known as **Taylorism** – in 1913 Henry Ford implemented his first assembly-line production of magneto flywheels. That same

Flywheel production
for *Model T*, 1914

year he developed a chassis-building system in which the chassis were pulled by rope past stockpiles of components, with the whole of the manufacturing process being compartmentalized into individual repetitive tasks. When the system was further improved with electrically-powered chain-drive movement, assembly time for the *Model T* was reduced from 12 hours and 8 minutes under the old system (in which parts were carried to a stationary assembly point) to just 1 hour and 33 minutes. Whereas *Model T* production figures for 1910 had stood at 20,000 units at a cost of $850 each, by 1916 this total had trebled to 60,000 units, at a cost of $360 each, clearly demonstrating the efficacy of the moving assembly line technique. When production of the *Model T* ceased in 1927, 15 million had rolled off Ford's assembly line and the company was now producing half of all the motor vehicles in the world. While the success of assembly-line mass production has always rested upon elaborate planning and synchronization, the meticulous design and **standardization** of components, and the efficiency of the overall design of the product, it has also depended heavily on large-scale investment in the plants and tooling required. Generally, only very large companies can afford to make such investments. Thus the rise of Fordism has precipitated the ascendancy of a small number of increasingly global corporations – from Boeing to IBM – who dominate their particular markets. More recently, demands for increased productivity have prompted the introduction of automated systems of mass production, with robots being increasingly employed for manufacturing processes that are repetitive, unpleasant and potentially injurious to human health, such as welding and spray painting, or which require handling of heavy and awkward workpieces or tools. Meanwhile, automation has been carried to a new level in the shape of computer-integrated manufacturing (CIM), which has evolved out of the

Gas tank desk for
Model T, 1914

use of **Computer-Aided Design** and **Computer-Aided Manufacturing** (CAD/
CAM) systems, and which now goes well beyond design and production to
include most of a firm's business functions. While the automation of Fordist
systems of production has resulted in the elimination of many unskilled
jobs, it has increased demand for knowledgeable technicians to oversee the
operation of automated devices. Against many expectations, automation
has led to the reappearance of the skilled worker. It has also improved efficiency and expanded production while relieving the drudgery and increasing
the earnings of the worker – exactly the aims of Frederick Winslow Taylor at
the turn of the 20th century.

FUNCTIONALISM

Functionalism is essentially an approach to architecture and design rather than a style, and is concerned with addressing practical problems as logically and efficiently as possible. The origins of Functionalism can be found in the theories of the first-century BC Roman architect, Vitruvius, which themselves were based on the Hellenistic tradition. The Classical or functional approach to architecture has since been revived many times: during the Renaissance in the 15th and 16th centuries, in the 18th century by Neo-Classical architects

Wilhelm Wagenfeld, *Sintrax* coffee maker for Jenaer Glaswerke Schott & Gen., 1931

and in the 19th century by luminaries such as Gottfried Semper and Eugène-Emmanuel Viollet-le-Duc. In the last half of the 19th century, design reformers in Britain such as A. W. N. Pugin and William Morris also advocated a functional approach to design, which led to the manufacture of utilitarian products. But it was the American architect Louis Sullivan who coined the expression "form follows function" in 1896 and who is therefore commonly credited with formulating 20th-century Functionalism. These early pioneers

Marcel Breuer, precursor of the *B5* chair, c. 1926 and *B3* chair for Standard-Möbel, later manufactured by Thonet, 1926–1927

of Functionalism promoted a methodology that took into consideration the
specific culture and environment of the region in which a design or building
was created. During the early half of the 20th century, however, **Modern
Movement** designers allied Functionalism with **Rationalism** and looked for
universal design solutions rather than national ones. The teaching at the
Staatliches **Bauhaus** in Dessau was founded on this quest and designers
such as Ludwig Mies van der Rohe, Marcel Breuer, Le Corbusier and J. J. P.
Oud experimented with industrial materials such as **tubular metal**, steel
and glass so as to create functional furniture and buildings. However, these
new materials were chosen by many as much for their modern machine-
aesthetic as for their functional potential. In the 1920s, the formal vocabulary of Functionalist design was evolved into a style, especially in France and
Germany, by **avant-garde** designers who were concerned with promoting
the appearance of modernity. By the 1930s, the Functionalist aesthetic had
become widely accepted, and ushered in the **International Style**. During
the 1960s, the social morality of Functionalism – which was seen by some
as mainly style-led – was questioned by **Anti-Design** groups and this in
turn gave rise to the emergence of **Post-Modernism**. Modernism in the
20th century has for the most part been affiliated with Functionalism and
Rationalism – terms that are virtually indistinguishable since they both pro-
pose a technologically driven logic of construction as the basis of design.

FUTURISM

ITALY

Fortunato Depero,
Design for a visiting
card for the Depero
Typographic Works,
1927

Futurism was founded in 1909 by the Italian writer Filippo Tommaso Marinetti. As its name suggests, the movement dissociated itself from the past by embracing technological progress. Marinetti's *Futurist Manifesto* of 1909 celebrated the inherent potential and dynamism of the machine and systems of communication. As the first cultural movement to distance itself from nature and to glorify the metropolis, Futurism was extremely influential to subsequent design movements. The energetic flux of modern city life was captured in the artistic works of Umberto Boccioni, Gino Severini, Carlo Carrà and Giacomo Balla through the use of fragmented Cubist-like geometric elements that evoked the feeling of speed and acceleration. Within graphic design, Futurism was asserted through the use of typography that was laid out expressively rather than conventionally. This idea of expressive structure was also used in the composition of poetry. In 1910, the *Manifesto of Futurist Painting* was signed by Carrà, Balla, Boccioni, Severini and Luigi Russolo, and later Balla became the first to experiment with the practical application of Futurist theory to the decorative arts. These expressive forays into design were followed up by the artist and designer, Fortunato Depero, who set up a craft workshop for Futurist art in Rovereto, which operated throughout the 1920s. Depero wrote the *Complessità plastica – gioco libero futurista – L'essere vivente-artificiale* (Plastic complexity – free futuristic play – the artificial-living being) in 1914 and at his House of Art in Rovereto he devised a neo-plastic language of design that was later promoted by the Italian Rationalists. The architect Antonio Sant'Elia joined the movement in 1914 and exhibited his proposals for "The New City" in Milan. The sweeping dynamic forms of his architecture were left unornamented and, with their raw unfinished surfaces and violent colouring, verged on Brutalism. Although Sant'Elia died in 1916, his *Manifesto for Futurist Architecture* remained influential, especially to members of **De Stijl** who received it in 1917. Futurism attempted to subvert bourgeois culture and was in some ways a destructive force in that it necessarily expressed the aggressive aesthetic of urban life in the machine-age. Aligned to Fascism, the Futurists sought order through radicalism and in so doing can be seen as the first truly **Radical Design** movement.

Fortunato Depero's
craft workshop for
Futurist art in
Rovereto, 1920

GESAMT-KUNSTWERK

Gesamtkunstwerk is a German term, which literally means "complete-art-work". Its use dates from the 19th century and refers to an amalgamation of all the arts. Originally, the concept of Gesamtkunstwerk was associated with the operas of Richard Wagner, which blended music with drama. Later, it was related to the notion of wholly integrated design in architecture and interiors whereby every element involved in an artistic scheme was meticulously designed, usually by a single creator. This idea of design unification was taken up most famously by architects aligned to the **Arts & Crafts Movement** such as Charles Rennie Mackintosh and Frank Lloyd Wright. They took the idea of the total work of art one step further by ensuring that their buildings were in complete harmony with the surrounding environment and were functionally appropriate. They also designed the smallest of details for their buildings and interiors, down to cutlery and door fittings. In Austria and Germany, Josef Hoffmann and Peter Behrens were also prominent exponents of the concept of Gesamtkunstwerk. The idea of completely unified design, as expressed through Gesamtkunstwerk, later influenced the practice of "total design" in which the design, manufacture and marketing of products is approached holistically.

Frank Lloyd Wright, dining room of
Hollyhock House, Los Angeles, designed
for Aline Barnsdall, 1917–1920

Design Council,
Kitemark, 1959

GOOD DESIGN

Good Design is a concept based on a rational approach to the design process whereby products are created in accordance with the formal, technical and aesthetic principles generally associated with the **Modern Movement**. In the late 1940s the criteria for products of Good Design were identified by D.J. De Pree, the founder of the Herman Miller Furniture Company, as durability, unity, integrity, inevitability and beauty. The Museum of Modern Art, New York staged the first Good Design exhibition in 1950, which was laid out by Charles and Ray Eames. The winning designs were selected by a three-man jury and were retailed through stores with an accompanying Good Design label. The premiss of Good Design was also favourably received in Europe, especially in Germany. In 1952, Max Bill co-founded the **Hochschule für Gestaltung**, **Ulm** to promote the virtues of Good Design that had previously been extolled at the **Bauhaus**. Bill was also responsible for the establishment of the "Die Gute Industrieform" exhibitions in Germany. The concept of Good Design was most notably embraced at Braun, where Dieter Rams developed a functionalist house-style for electrical products. In Britain, Good Design was actively promoted by the Design Council (founded in 1960) through exhibitions and its journal *Design*. The Council implemented the use of its famous "kitemark" label as a seal of approval for worthy products. In the 1960s there was a reaction against the conservative conformity of Good Design and what was seen as the Establishment's dictation of "good taste". The popular reaction to Good Design ushered in **Post-Modernism**, which brought radicalism, emotion, spontaneity and character back into mainstream design.

HIGH-TECH

The High Tech style first emerged in architecture in the mid-1960s and was inspired by the geometric formalism of classical Modernism and the **Radical Design** proposals of Buckminster Fuller. The utilitarianism underlying the style countered the excesses of **Pop Design**. Pioneered by British architects such as Norman Foster, Richard Rogers and Michael Hopkins, who incorporated unadorned industrial elements into their buildings, the High Tech style eventually found its way into mainstream interior design during the 1970s. Utilitarian equipment and fittings manufactured for factory and institutional use, such as trolleys, rubber flooring, clip-on lighting, galvanized zinc shelving and scaffolding poles were used in High Tech interiors, which often included primary colour schemes in homage to **De Stijl**. In America, exponents of High-Tech included Joseph Paul D'Urso and Ward Bennett, who worked with salvaged industrial materials. In 1978, Joan Kron and Susan Slesin published a book entitled *High-Tech: The Industrial Style and Source Book for the Home*, but by this time the style was already waning and was superseded in the early 1980s by **Post-Modernism**. The promotion of industrial components through High Tech did, however, inspire British designers such as Ron Arad and Tom Dixon in the mid-1980s to create poetic "One-Off" designs from salvaged materials including scaffolding poles, car seats and manhole covers.

Michael Hopkins,
Hopkins House
studio, 1979

HOCHSCHULE FÜR GESTALTUNG, ULM

1953–1968
ULM, GERMANY

The Hochschule für Gestaltung was founded in 1953 in Ulm, Germany, by Otl Aicher and Inge Scholl with the aim of reviving the socially inspired teaching of the **Bauhaus**, halted by the National Socialists in the 1930s. The idea for a new design school arose through a meeting with Max Bill in 1947, who subsequently designed the institution's buildings and became its first director. The courses began in 1953, with various ex-Bauhaus staff including Ludwig Mies van der Rohe, Josef Albers and Johannes Itten becoming visiting teachers. The school buildings were opened in 1955, and the following year the Argentinian design theorist, Tomás Maldonado assumed the directorship. Although the school humanized design methodology with courses on **semiotics**, anthropology, contextual study and psychology, it is best remembered for **Functionalism** and a systematic approach to design reliant on engineering. The resulting industrial aesthetic profoundly influenced German product design, as epitomised by the work of Hans Gugelot and Dieter Rams for Braun. In 1968, a year after Maldonado, who called for "mass production, mass communication, mass participation", had left the HfG, local authorities withdrew funding, declaring that the institution was too radical. Shortly afterwards, the staff decided to close the school often referred to as "the new Bauhaus". While some staff members had approached product design systematically and scientifically – for instance Hans Gugelot, director of the product design department from 1954 – others had ventured to reject dogmatic Functionalism. It was this fundamental contradiction that thwarted not only the Hochschule für Gestaltung, but also its spiritual predecessor, the Bauhaus.

Uppercase 5 edited by Theo Crosby, 1961 – a selection of essays by Tomás Maldonado outlining the Hochschule für Gestaltung's rational approach to design

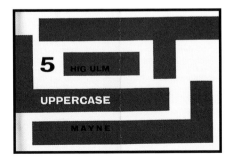

INDEPENDENT GROUP

FOUNDED 1952
LONDON, GREAT BRITAIN

Formed in 1952, the Independent Group held regular meetings at the ICA (Institute of Contemporary Art) in London to examine the technical achievements of American industrial production and the emergence of popular consumerist culture. The group, which included Richard Hamilton, Eduardo Paolozzi, Reyner Banham and Peter and Alison Smithson, rejected Modernist philosophy and drew inspiration from "low" rather than "high" art. As protagonists of popular culture, certain members of the Independent Group championed the idea of built-in obsolescence, which was naively seen as beneficial for the economic growth it offered through increased production. Significantly, in his collage of 1956 entitled *Just what is it that makes today's homes so different, so appealing?*, Hamilton incorporated an image of a lollypop bearing the word "POP". This was possibly the first time that a word used in a work of art became the label for a new art movement. Certainly, this landmark work heralded a new direction not only in art but also in design. Hamilton identified the characteristics of Pop as – "Popular (designed for a mass audience), Transient (short-term solution), Expendable (easily forgotten), Low Cost, Mass Produced, Young (aimed at youth), Witty, Sexy, Gimmicky, Glamorous, Big Business". By defining Pop and raising the status of popular culture to a subject of serious academic interest, the Independent Group laid the theoretical foundations upon which **Pop Design** was to flourish in the 1960s.

Richard Hamilton,
Just what is it that makes today's homes so different, so appealing? Collage, 1956

INDUSTRIAL DESIGN

Marcello Nizzoli,
Lettera 22 typewriter
for Olivetti, 1950

For over 200 years, the products of mechanized industrial production have shaped our material culture, influenced world economies and affected the quality of our environment and daily lives. From consumer goods and **packaging** to transportation systems and production equipment, industrial products encompass an extraordinary range of functions, techniques, attitudes, ideas and values and are a means through which we experience and perceive the world around us. The nature of industrial products and how they come to be is determined by an ever more complex process of design that is itself subject to many different influences and factors. Not least of these are the constraints imposed by the social, economic, political, cultural, organizational, and commercial contexts within which new products are developed, and the character, thinking and creative abilities of the individual designers or teams of designers, aligned specialists and manufacturers involved in their realization. Industrial design – the conception and planning of products for multiple reproduction – is a creative and inventive process concerned with the synthesis of such instrumental factors as engineering, technology, materials and aesthetics into machine-producible solutions that balance all user needs

Peter Behrens,
electric tea kettle for
AEG, 1909

and desires within technical and social constraints. Engineering – the application of scientific principles to the design and construction of structures, machines, apparatus or manufacturing processes – is an essential and defining aspect of industrial design. While both disciplines are concerned with finding optimum solutions to specific problems, the primary distinguishing characteristic of industrial design is its concern for aesthetics. The origins of industrial design can be traced back to the Industrial Revolution, which began in Great Britain in the mid-18th century and which heralded the era of mechanization. Prior to this, objects were craft-produced, whereby both the conception and the manufacture of an object were the work of a single individual. With the development of new industrial manufacturing processes and the division of labour, design (concep-

Florian Seiffert,
Aromaster KF 20
coffee maker for
Braun, 1972

tion and planning) was progressively separated from the act of making. At this early stage, however, design had no intellectual, theoretical or philosophical foundation and was considered just one of the many interrelated aspects of mechanical production. Thus the industrial goods of the years up to the 19th century were created by specialists from the technical, materials and production spheres rather than by an industrial designer. Towards the end of the 19th century, however, manufacturers began to realise that they could gain a critical competitive advantage by improving the constructional integrity and aesthetic appearance of their products. As a consequence, they began to invite specialists from other spheres– most notably, architects – to contribute to the design process. Industrial design subsequently became a fully-fledged discipline in the early 20th century, when design theory was integrated into industrial methods of production. Among the first professional industrial design practitioners was the German architect Peter Behrens, who was recruited by AEG in 1907 to improve the company's products and **corporate identity**. Since then, industrial design has become an increasingly important factor in the success of industrial products and the companies that manufacture them. While the aim of the industrial designer has always been to strike the best possible balance between the intellectual, functional, emotional, aesthetic and ethical expectations of the user/consumer and the influences and factors bearing upon the design process, it is important to remember that, historically, without the willingness of manufacturers to risk the necessary and sometimes massive investments demanded by the development of new products, there would be very little industrial design.

INSTITUTE OF DESIGN, CHICAGO

FOUNDED 1944
CHICAGO, USA

Photograph of
the New Bauhaus
building in Chicago,
1937

In 1933, the Staatliches **Bauhaus** in Dessau was closed by the Nazi regime, who declared it a subversive institution, forcing many of its teaching staff to emigrate so as to escape persecution. Having first settled in London, László Moholy-Nagy moved to Chicago in 1937, on the invitation of the Association of Arts and Industries, to organize a new design school that would invigorate the cultural and economic life of that city. Based on the teaching principles of its German antecedent, the "New Bauhaus" as it was dubbed by Moholy-Nagy, attempted to promote a culture of "total education". The new school, however, was short-lived, the Association withdrawing its funding in the last few months of 1938, because they found its programme too experimental. The following year, Moholy-Nagy re-opened the institution with the private backing of Walter Papecke, the chairman of the Container Corporation of America, and it was rechristened the Chicago School of Design. In 1944 the school acquired its current title, the Institute of Design, and after the death of Moholy-Nagy in 1946 it became a department of the Armour Institute, which was itself renamed the Illinois Institute of Technology. That same year, the Russian émigré designer Serge Chermayeff succeeded Moholy-Nagy as director of the school. From its earliest beginnings, the Institute of Design approached design teaching from an experimental standpoint and the original curriculum included not only design studies but also courses in psychology and literature. Today, the Institute of Design remains dedicated to "pushing the boundaries of design" and specializes in the application of new technologies within the design process.

Jacobus Johannes
Pieter Oud, *Giso 405*
table lamp for
Gispen, 1928

Le Corbusier, Pierre
Jeanneret and
Charlotte Perriand,
dining room
exhibited at the
Salon des Artistes
Décorateurs in Paris,
1928

INTERNATIONAL STYLE

The term International Style was first coined in 1931 by
Alfred H. Barr Jr., the director of the Museum of Modern
Art, New York, for the title of a catalogue, *International
Style: Architecture Since 1922*, which accompanied Henry-
Russell Hitchcock's and Philip Johnson's landmark exhibition of 1932. In the work of Modernists such as Le
Corbusier, Jacobus Johannes Pieter Oud, Walter Gropius
and Ludwig Mies van der Rohe, Barr identified a univer-
sal style that transcended national borders – the like of which had not been
seen in Western art and architecture since the Middle Ages, when the so-
called International Gothic Style had flourished across Europe. The new
20th-century movement was named accordingly in tribute to this earlier
precedent. The term International Style referred specifically to the work of
Modern Movement architects and designers, who married function and
technology with a geometric vocabulary of form to produce a pared-down
Modern aesthetic. Although it is sometimes used to describe early Modernism (c. 1900 to 1933) and the work of designers such as Adolf Loos and
J. J. P. Oud, it is now generally associated with the less utilitarian form of
Modernism that emerged after the closure of the **Bauhaus** in 1933. The term
also refers to the work of Le Corbusier and his followers, who during the
late 1920s and 1930s promoted a more stylish and less austere version of
Modernism. Perhaps the greatest exponents of the International Style, how-

ever, were Ludwig Mies van der
Rohe and Walter Gropius, who having emigrated to the United States,
tirelessly attempted to "internation-
alize" the Modern Movement not
only through their architectural
commissions and exhibitions but
through their high profile teaching
positions in America during the
post-war years. Many advocates
of the International Style adopted
the Functionalist aesthetic of the

↑ **Le Corbusier,
Pierre Jeanneret and
Charlotte Perriand**,
*Model No. B301
Basculant* chair for
Thonet, c. 1928

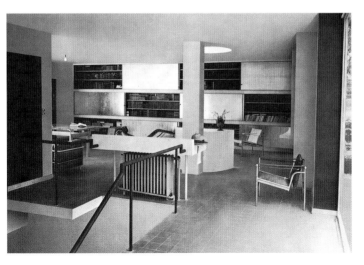

Le Corbusier, library
in the Church House
at Ville d'Avray,
1928–1929

Le Corbusier,
**Pierre Jeanneret and
Charlotte Perriand,**
Model No. B306
chaise longue for
Thonet, 1928
(reissued by Cassina)

Modern Movement for purely stylistic reasons. Others, however, developed an aesthetic purity so as to promote a greater universalism in architecture and design. Later post-war designers – especially in America – such as Florence Knoll, Charles Eames and George Nelson married this modern and democratic approach to design with methods of industrial mass-production so as to create products that fulfilled all the criteria of **Good Design**. During the 1920s and 1930s, the International Style in architecture and interior design was characterized by geometric formalism, the use of industrial materials such as steel and glass and a widespread preference for white rendering. Later, some architects and designers, including Eero Saarinen and Charles Eames, sought to humanize the International Style through the adoption of sculptural forms and the contrasting of geometric and organic shapes, while Kenzo Tange and others took the International Style to its logical conclusion in the creation of Brutalism, an architectural style that employs dehumanizing materials and treatments such as exposed rough-cast concrete and rigid geometry. Although it appeared in the late 1970s and 1980s that the emergence of **Post-Modernism** had tolled the death knell of the International Style, by the late 1980s and 1990s architects such as Norman Foster and Richard Rogers were winning acclaim for their highly engineered buildings, which bore the unmistakable characteristics of the International Style –

Florence Knoll,
The *Florence Knoll
Collection – 1205S1*
lounge chair, *1205S2*
two-seater sofa,
1205S3 three-seater
sofa and *2511T*
table – for Knoll
International, 1954

power, elegance and clarity. In recent years, there has also been a return to a rational aesthetic within product and furniture design, as manufacturers seek global solutions that, like the International Style, are trans-cultural. The term International Style can therefore refer to a very specific period and type of Modernism, while also alluding to the aesthetics resulting from a Functionalist approach to design, the ancestry of which can be traced back to the earliest beginnings of the Modern Movement.

JUGENDSTIL

GERMANY

Otto Eckmann,
stoneware vase with
bronze mount,
c. 1900

Jugendstil translates literally as "Youth Style" and refers
to the branch of **Art Nouveau** that emerged in Germany
during the 1890s. The term was derived from the title
of the magazine *Jugend*, which was founded in Munich
by Georg Hirth in 1896 and did much to popularize
the new style. Inspired by the reforming ideas of John
Ruskin and William Morris, Jugendstil designers such
as Hermann Obrist, Richard Riemerschmid and August
Endell had more idealistic aims than other proponents of the Art Nouveau
style in Europe. They not only sought to reform art but also advocated a
return to a simpler and less commercial way of life. They possessed a youthful optimism and a reverence for nature that was expressed vigourously
through their work. Like their contemporaries in Brussels and Paris, Jugendstil designers were inspired by the workings of the natural world as revealed
through advances in scientific research and technology. The swirling vegetal motifs and whiplash forms employed by August Endell and Hermann
Obrist, for example, were directly influenced by Karl Blossfeldt's photographic studies of plant structures, which depicted remarkable spiral growth
patterns, and by the botanical drawings of Ernst Haeckel. The new understanding of nature provided by detailed analyses such as these helped
Jugendstil designers to capture a sense of dynamism and energetic organic
growth in their work. In Germany, this new ahistorical style challenged the
official imperial art policy emanating from Berlin, and regions wishing to
express their sense of cultural autonomy, such as Dresden, Munich, Darmstadt, Weimar and Hagen, embraced Jugendstil wholeheartedly. Although
this desire for artistic independence was a theme that united the emerging
schools of Art Nouveau in other European cities such as Brussels, Nancy
and even Glasgow, it was perhaps felt most strongly across Germany.
Jugendstil designers came closer than any of their European contemporaries associated with Art Nouveau to bridging the gulf that existed between
"artistic manufacture" and industrial production. Many workshops were
established to produce their reformed designs, most notably the Vereinigte
Werkstätten für Kunst im Handwerk (United Workshops for Artist Craftsmanship) in 1897 and the Dresdener Werkstätten für Handwerkskunst

August Endell,
design for the boxes
in the Buntes
Theater in Berlin,
1901

(Dresden Workshops for Artist Craftsmanship) in 1898. These ventures were set up with the objective of producing honest domestic wares through ethical manufacturing practices. The objects produced in Dresden were less elaborate and hence less expensive than those manufactured in Munich but were still beyond the means of the average householder. Richard Riemerschmid, chief designer at the Dresden workshop, adopted a simple vernacular style that was similar to the work of British Arts & Crafts designers such as Charles Voysey. Riemerschmid sought to reform design through **standardization** and his adoption of rational manufacturing practices at the Dresdener Werkstätten für Handwerkskunst was extremely influential, contributing to the founding of the **Deutscher Werkbund**. The Vereinigte Werkstätten für Kunst im Handwerk, which were founded in Munich by Bruno Paul and others, also played a key role in the promotion of Jugendstil. Paul designed boldly outlined cartoons and graphics for the journal *Simplicissimus,* which, like the magazine *Jugend*, popularized the new aesthetic. His linear style was shared by his fellow Munich designer Bernhard Pankok, whose Lange house in Tübingen (1902) was conceived as a **Gesamtkunstwerk**. The building was influenced by vernacularism, as were the Jugendstil interiors, which were startlingly modern in their simplicity. In Darmstadt, the Jugendstil cause was heavily patronized by Grand Duke Ernst Ludwig of

Darmstadt-Hesse who instigated an exhibition entitled, "Ein Dokument Deutscher Kunst" (A Document of German Art) in 1901. The exhibition celebrated the artistic achievements of the Darmstädter Künstlerkolonie (Darmstadt Artists' Colony), which had been established with the Grand Duke's private funding in 1899. The Darmstädter Künstlerkolonie initially comprised eight buildings including Josef Maria Olbrich's "House for Decorative Art" studio building and seven artists' residences built for members of the colony. The Darmstädter Künstlerkolonie was not only important for the new civic architectural style it promoted, which embraced Jugendstil, but also for its encouragement of the manufacture of art works. In Weimar, the promotion of Jugendstil was similarly prompted by both civic pride and economic necessity and also received ducal patronage. In 1860, the Grand Duke Karl Alexander of Saxony-Weimar privately funded the establishment of an art school in Weimar. He was succeeded by his grandson in 1901 who was persuaded by Count Harry Kessler to appoint the Belgian architect Henry van de Velde as art counsellor to his court. The belief that the local economy would be boosted through art education eventually led to van de Velde's being commissioned to design the Weimar Kunstgewerbeschule (School of Applied Arts) in 1904. He directed the institution until 1914, and during his tenure, produced many Jugendstil designs for silverware and ceramics that were remarkable for their simplicity of form. Jugendstil architec-

Covered bowl,
Munich, c. 1900

ture and design often united structural innovation with abstracted naturalistic forms to produce an extraordinary combination of monumentality and visual lightness. The style reached its zenith around 1900 and was shortly afterwards superseded by the industrial rationalism of the Deutscher Werkbund, founded in 1907 by a group of designers and architects who had been affiliated with Jugendstil. Through its promotion of natural forms and "folk" types as a means of reforming design and ultimately society, Jugendstil had much in common with the British **Arts & Crafts Movement**, while its adoption of more industrialized methods of production paved the way for later developments in German design. The term "Jugendstil" can also be used to refer to Austrian and Scandinavian Art Nouveau.

Ferdinand Morawe, clock for the Vereinigte Werkstätten für Kunst im Handwerk, 1903

1896 · 21. MÄRZ · JUGEND · I. JAHRGANG · NR. 12

JUGEND

MÜNCHNER
ILLUSTR.
WOCHENSCHRIFT
FÜR KUNST & LEBEN.

QUARTALPREIS 3 MARK.
PREIS DER NUMMER 30 PFG.

VERLAG VON G. HIRTH, MÜNCHEN.

Herausgeber: Georg Hirth. — Redakteur: Fritz v. Ostini. — Alle Rechte vorbehalten.

KITSCH

Selection of
umbrella stands,
late 1950s

Selection of umbrella stands, late 1950s

The term Kitsch derives from the German verb "verkitschen" (to cheapen) and is used to describe vulgarized designs that have a popular appeal. Kitsch has therefore come to be seen as the very antithesis of **Good Design**. The term was originally used to describe non-functional items such as souvenirs, knick-knacks and novelties. One of the first studies on the subject was by the German philosopher Fritz Karpfen in his publication of 1925, entitled *Der Kitsch*. However, it was not until the American art critic Clement Greenberg wrote *Kitsch and the Avantgarde* in 1939 that its meaning was widened to define elements of contemporary popular culture, such as commercial advertising and "trashy" literature. In the 1950s, Kitsch design reached its zenith with manufacturer's producing "knock-off" products that bore only a passing resemblance to the "high" design artefacts that had inspired them. During this period, a plethora of cheap and tacky products was produced, often in **plastics**, that relied on gimmickry and an element of humour for their appeal. This phenomenon was spurred on by popular consumerism and can be seen as a reaction against the state and institutional promotion of Good Design. During the 1960s, Kitsch continued to be used as a derogatory term, but by the 1970s, Kitsch objects were being used ironically in interiors and were knowingly appreciated for their self-conscious bad taste. With the emergence of **Post-Modernism** in the 1980s, Kitsch became lauded for its cultural honesty and its subversive tendencies. Through its mocking of "good taste", Kitsch had at last found fertile ground within the **avant-garde**.

MEDICAL DESIGN

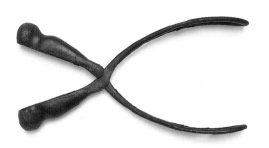

Inhaler, Great Britian, late 19th century

Medical design falls into three broad categories: prosthetics, products designed for the administration of drugs, and equipment created for diagnostic purposes or medical therapies. Throughout the history of medicine, new designs have been devised to assist in the treatment of the sick and the disabled. It was not until the early 18th century, however, that accurate anatomical studies began to directly inform medical design. At this stage, the universities in Edinburgh and Glasgow led the world in anatomical research and it was a Scotsman, William Smellie, who designed the first modern obstetric forceps. Once in position, the two sections of this revolutionary design locked together so as to effectively cradle the baby's head. It is a tribute to Smellie's invention that the forceps used in today's hospitals differ little from his original design. During the 18th and 19th centuries, industrialization fuelled the growth of urban populations and with them the rise of infectious diseases like tuberculosis, typhoid and diphtheria. Respiratory diseases were often made worse by airborne pollution from domestic fires and coal-burning factories. The thick fogs common to so many cities during Victorian times were disastrous to the health of inhabitants, and most households would have owned a ceramic inhaler as it offered one of the best forms of medical treatment prior to the advent of antibiotics. The greatest benefits to health, however, were not advanced by medical design or new drugs but by the implementation of proper sanitation systems from the mid-1800s onwards. This period

Obstetrical forceps, c. 1820 – based on a revolutionary design created by William Smellie in 1752

also saw the advent of modern industrialized warfare, which resulted in an unprecedented need for **design for disability** and in particular prosthetics. Since the beginning of the 20th century, technological advances have often found life-saving applications within the field of medicine, as evidenced by medical X-ray equipment, for example. When a new medical typology is introduced,

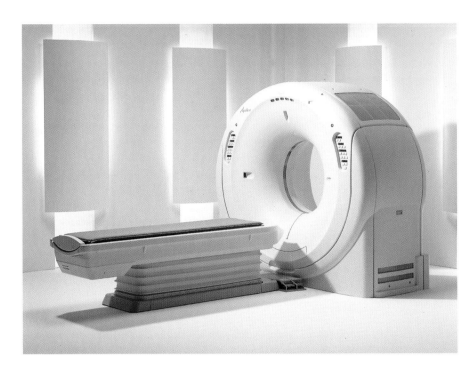

its design may appear relatively unrefined because it is informed almost entirely by technology. As the typology evolves, however, its design will become user-friendlier and less threatening in appearance. Thus the brain scanner first introduced in 1970–1971 has today metamorphosed into the **soft-tech** *Aquilion* CT scanner (1997) designed by Masahiko Kitayama for Toshiba. Increasingly, designers are also helping to develop better ways of administering drugs, such as Weston Medical's needle-free injector or the *HandiHaler* asthma inhaler (1995) designed by Kinneir Dufort for Boehringer. With the emphasis today firmly on human-centric design, a host of bio-compatible designs are being implanted into the human body to replace worn-out body parts – from pace-makers to high-tech ceramic hip replacements. Although medical design is by necessity driven by function rather than aesthetics, designers and manufacturers are increasingly realising that the appearance of medical equipment can have a psychological effect upon patients and can thereby influence – and potentially enhance – the therapeutic value of a design solution.

MEMPHIS

FOUNDED 1981
MILAN, ITALY

Martine Bedine,
Super lamp for
Memphis, 1981

Memphis was founded in Milan in 1981 with the aim of re-invigorating the **Radical Design** movement. During the late 1970s, **avant-garde** Italian designers such as Ettore Sottsass, Andrea Branzi and Alessandro Mendini, and other members of Studio Alchimia, experimented with alternative artistic and intellectual approaches to design. Mendini's promotion of "re-design" and "banal design" became central to the output of Studio Alchimia, and Sottsass, who found these approaches too creatively restricting, eventually left the group. On the 11th of December 1980, Sottsass hosted a gathering at his house of designers such as Barbara Radice, Michele De Lucchi, Marco Zanini, Aldo Cibic, Matteo Thun and Martine Bedin to discuss the need for a new creative approach to design. They decided to form a design collaborative, and that very night it was christened Memphis, after a Bob Dylan song entitled "Stuck Inside of Mobile with the Memphis Blues Again", which had been played repeatedly throughout the evening. The name, Memphis, also made reference to the ancient Egyptian capital of culture and the Tennessee birthplace of Elvis Presley and was therefore suitably "double-coded". The group,

Masanori Umeda,
Tawaraya boxing ring
conversation pit for
Memphis, 1981

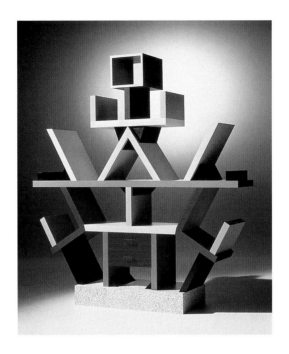

now including Nathalie du Pasquier and George Sowden, convened again
in February 1981, by which time its members had executed over a hundred
drawings of bold and colourful designs, drawing inspiration from either
futuristic themes or past decorative styles including **Art Deco** and 1950s
Kitsch, and intentionally mocking the pretensions of **Good Design**. They
threw themselves into the project: finding furniture and ceramics manufacturers willing to batch produce their designs; convincing Abet to make new
laminates printed with extraordinarily vibrant patterns inspired by Pop Art,
Op Art and electronic imagery; designing and producing promotional material and so on. The head of Artemide, Ernesto Gismondi, subsequently
became the president of Memphis, and on the 18th of September 1981 the
group showed its work for the first time at the Arc '74 showroom in Milan.
The furniture, lighting, clocks and ceramics exhibited by Memphis had been
designed by an international array of architects and designers including
Hans Hollein, Shiro Kuramata, Peter Shire, Javier Mariscal, Massanori
Umeda and Michael Graves. The group's products caused an immediate
sensation, not least owing to their blatant **Anti-Design** agenda, and the
same year, the book *Memphis, The New International Style* was published as
a means of promoting their work. Artemide, which produced Memphis'

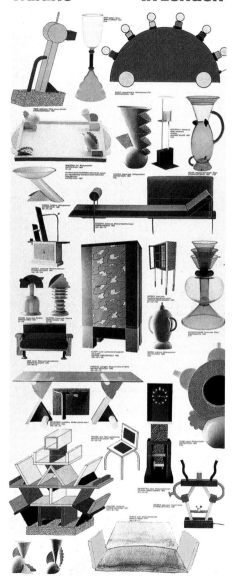

Brochure for
"Memphis Milano
in London"
exhibition held at
The Boilerhouse,
Victoria & Albert
Museum, 1982

Ettore Sottsass,
Mizar vase for
Memphis, 1982

1982 designs, gave the group space to display their products at the company's showroom on Corso Europa, Milan. From 1981 to 1988, Barbara Radice was art director of Memphis and organized exhibitions in London, Chicago, Düsseldorf, Edinburgh, Geneva, Hanover, Jerusalem, Los Angeles, Montreal, New York, Paris, Stockholm and Tokyo. Many of Memphis' monumental designs used colourful plastic laminates, a material favoured for its "lack of culture". The vibrancy, eccentricity and ornamentation of Memphis' output evolved from a knowledge of Modernism and then an utter rejection of it. The hybrid themes and oblique quotations of past styles used by Memphis produced a new Post-Modern vocabulary of design. The group always acknowledged that Memphis was a "fad", tied to the ephemerality of fashion, and in 1988, when its popularity began to wane, Sottsass disbanded it. Although a short-lived phenomena, Memphis, with its youthful vitality and humour, was central to the internationalization of **Post-Modernism**.

MILITARY DESIGN

Ludwig Hohlwein, poster for Motoren-fabrik Oberusel, Germany, 1910s

While the effectiveness of military weaponry and hardware is perpetually improved as a result of technological progress, the primary criteria for military design have remained the same for centuries, namely durability, strength, fitness for purpose, functionality, transportability, ease of maintenance and repair, and rationalized/standardized construction for ease of manufacture.

How well a weapon functions is often a decisive factor in war, and so in order to gain the advantage over an enemy it is essential to have the latest equipment available. This factor has led to the culture of continuous development within military design – a realm of many specializations that can be broken down into five main categories: offensive weapons, defensive weapons, transportation, communications and detection systems. Although advanced technologies such as railways and telegraphy were used for military purposes in the 19th century, very few technological innovations were incorporated into the design of weapons during this period. Many modern manufacturing techniques, however, found their first application in the manufacture of small arms. In 1800 Eli Whitney developed a musket with interchangeable parts which heralded the advent of industrial **standardization**, while other small arms manufacturers in the United States, most notably the Springfield Armory, mass-produced rifles using mechanization

Major Wilson and **Sir William Tritton**, *Big Willie* tank, 1915

and the industrial division of labour. The mass production of weapons changed the face of military conflict forever, with the American Civil War being effectively the first example of modern (i.e. industrialized) warfare. By the outbreak of the First World War, weaponry had become relatively sophisticated and infinitely more deadly. The First World War saw the introduction of many "firsts", including the use of chemical weapons (such as mustard gas), aeroplanes for bombing, submarines and tanks. This war, however, was first and foremost an artillery conflict, and the quick-firing Howitzer field gun, with its high angle of fire, significantly outperformed older designs with flatter firing trajectories. WWI also saw the introduction of trench mortars and the development of primitive radio communications. During the Second World War, military designs that had been introduced in the earlier conflict were considerably improved. Battlefield communications became increasingly sophisticated and the design of field telephones enabled much better command and control of troops. The aircraft carrier also came of age and brought a completely new dimension to naval warfare, while the design of aircraft became increasingly specialized. Daylight bombers such as the Boeing *B-17 Flying Fortress* (1934–1935), for example, required the development of long-range escort fighters such as the North American *P-51 Mustang* (1940). Tanks also played an important role in providing armies with greater manoeuvrability and the possibility of

Interior of a shell-filling factory, Great Britain, c. 1915

M4 Sherman tank, 1942

punching holes through enemy lines – with its superior protection and fire-power, the Russian *T34* tank (1940) was among the most decisive weapons of WWII. The development of atomic weapons and the subsequent onset of the Cold War spawned a phenomenal proliferation of weapons and weapons systems, each progressively more sophisticated and deadly while at the same time more costly. This escalation was largely driven in the West by the American military-industrial complex – the powerful economic and political conjunction of the US military establishment, government officials and the defence industry. The collapse of Soviet Russia threatened to destabilise this alliance – though not before the US Air Force had taken possession of the hugely expensive, radar-deflecting "Stealth" family of fighter planes and bombers. Since then, however, the US military and its contractors have successfully argued that post-Cold War threats require new weapons systems. Conflicts in Iraq, Afghanistan and the Balkans have hastened the development of so-called "smart" munitions and unmanned reconnaissance planes. Above all, though, quantum leaps have been made in military communications and imaging, supported by powerful satellite technologies. The goal of battlefield connectivity – with commanders able to access real-time displays of their, and their opponents' assets – has been reached. The armed forces of other nations have, by and large, done what they can to keep pace.

MINIATURIZATION

Gerhard Fuchs, *Titan Minimal Art Model 7373* eyewear for Silhouette, 1999

As technology has evolved throughout the Modern era there has been an increasing trend towards miniaturization. The benefits of reducing the scale of industrially manufactured products are clear – weight, volume, unit costs to the manufacturer, costs to the user/consumer and the amount of waste generated can all be significantly decreased. Not surprisingly, the aerospace and automobile industries were among the first to explore the potential of miniaturization. Cars such as the Volkswagen *Beetle* (1934), Fiat 500 (1936), Fiat *Nuova 500* (1957) and Alec Issigonis' *Mini* (1959) were not only among the smallest cars produced in their time, but were also the least expensive and the most popular. The extraordinary advances made in the field of semiconductors during the mid-20th century led to the radical miniaturization of consumer electronics. 1947 saw the development of the first transistor by John Bardeen, Walter Brattain and William Shockley at the Bell Telephone Laboratories, heralding what many regarded as the "second industrial revolution". By the late 1950s the transistor had been perfected to such an extent that it began rapidly replacing the use of electron tubes – thereby allowing industrial designers the possibility of developing more compact electronic equipment; such as the world's first pocket-sized transistor radio, which was introduced by Sony in 1957. Another turning-point came with the development of the first integrated circuit by Jack St. Clair Kirby at Texas Instruments in 1958. Such revolutionary microchip technology enabled appliances to become more com-

Model WQV-1 wrist camera for Casio, 2000

pact, and easier to handle, transport and store. The bulky desktop calculator was soon replaced by pocket models, while the room-filling mainframe computers of the late 1950s and early 1960s eventually gave way to desktop personal computers in the 1980s and laptop computers in the 1990s. Today, we are surrounded by mini-versions of every imaginable product, from micro-

DaimlerChrysler MCC, *Smart Car*, introduced 1998

vehicles such as the *Smart Car* (1998) to the digital cameras (2000) by Casio which can be worn on the wrist. Minimal designs are also being made possible by new materials, such as the strong yet lightweight titanium employed in the wire-like eyewear produced by Silhouette. With the rapid development of "molecular electronics" and nanotechnology, the reduction in size of electronic devices will open the door to whole new classes of ultra-miniaturized products and information systems. It has been predicted that, in the 21st century, computing will be an automatic constituent of everyday objects across a wide range of product types.

MODERN MOVEMENT

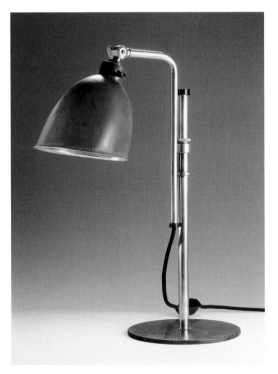

The Modern Movement in design was driven by a progressive and socially motivated ideology, the origins of which can be traced to the mid-19th century and the moral crusade of design reformers such as A. W. N. Pugin, John Ruskin and William Morris. These early pioneers recognized that the prevailing High Victorian style was the product of a society corrupted by greed, decadency and oppression, and strove to reform society through a new approach to design. Although forsaking industrial production in favour of handcraftsmanship, Morris was amongst the first to put theory into practice by producing holistically conceived, well-designed and executed objects for everyday use. His reforming ideas – the supremacy of utility, simplicity and appropriateness over luxury; the moral responsibility of designers and manufacturers to produce objects of quality, and the proposition that design could and should be used as a democratic tool for social change – had a fundamental impact on the development of the Modern Movement. His ideas stimulated the foundation of craft-based guilds and workshops in Britain, Germany and America that were more receptive to machine production. Increasingly, it was seen that the machine offered a means to an end and that the industrial process would have to be embraced wholeheartedly if reform was to be widespread. The founding of the **Deutscher Werkbund** in 1907 marked the point in time when reforming ideology met industrial production. Members of the Deutscher Werkbund developed

Christian Dell,
coffee pot,
c. 1929/1930

Christian Dell,
Rondella desk lamp
for Rondella,
1927–1928

a new and highly rational approach to design that eliminated ornament and stressed **Functionalism**. By eradicating superfluous surface decoration, elements were simplified and better **standardization** was achieved, which in turn promoted greater efficiency in terms of production and materials. The "saving" this approach offered benefited both the user and manufacturer as more value could go into the quality of construction and materials. The aesthetic purification that resulted from the modern approach to design provided a universal language of design that was intended to be impervious to fashion. Adolf Loos' famous publication, *Ornament und Verbrechen* (*Ornament and Crime*) of 1908, linked excessive decoration to the debasing of society, while a later Werkbund publication of 1924 entitled *Form ohne Orna-*

Alvar Aalto, *Model No. 31* armchair for Huonekalu-ja Rakennustyötehdas (later manufactured by Artek), 1930–1931

BAUHAUSBÜCHER

SCHRIFTLEITUNG:
WALTER GROPIUS
L. MOHOLY-NAGY

DIE
BÜHNE
IM
BAUHAUS

4

DIE
BÜHNE
IM
BAUHAUS

ALBERT LANGEN VERLAG
MÜNCHEN

László Moholy-Nagy,
title pages for Walter
Gropius and László
Moholy-Nagy's *Die
Bühne im Bauhaus –*
Bauhausbuch 4,
1925

ment (*Form without Ornament*) illustrated and expressed the virtues of plain
and rationally based designs for industrial production. This purging of ornament was also promoted by **De Stijl**, while **Constructivism** and **Futurism** celebrated the machine and the concept of "production art". After the devastation of the First World War, designers such as Walter Gropius recognized
the moral imperative of Modernism. Gropius became the first director of
the **Bauhaus**, which was established in 1919 to bring unity to the arts and
to put the reforming ideals of the early pioneers of Modernism into practice.
As the single most important design institution of the 20th century, the
Bauhaus had an enormous impact on the development of the Modern
Movement through its promotion of functionalism, industrial methods of
production and state-of-the-art materials, such as **tubular metal**. The functional efficiency of Bauhaus interiors, furniture, metalware, **ceramics** and
graphics led to a coherent vocabulary of design that became synonymous
with Modernism. The German term, Sachlichkeit (Objectivity) described this
new rational approach to design. However, by 1927, when the "Werkbund-
Ausstellung" was held in Stuttgart, a clearly identifiable **International Style** of
Modernism had emerged that was distinguished by **essentialism**, industrialism and rectilinearism. Le Corbusier played a key role in promoting this reductivist machine aesthetic, although his designs were significantly less util-

itarian than those produced at the Bauhaus. In the 1930s, the International Style became driven by fashion and was thought by some to have perverted the social objectives of Modernism. Exponents of the International Style took geometric abstraction to extremes and employed industrial materials and a severe formal vocabulary for stylistic purposes. Modernism appeared to have lost its moral bearings until it was taken up by Scandinavian designers, most notably Alvar Aalto, who pioneered a humanizing form of Modernism through **Organic Design**. Aalto's work was especially well received in Britain and America and inspired a new generation of Modern Movement designers, such as Charles and Ray Eames, to perpetuate a holistic and organic approach to design that embraced state-of-the-art technologies and materials. Although the achievements and future relevance of Modernism have been debated for decades, its fundamental moral democratic premise cannot be refuted.

Alvar Aalto,
discussion and
lecture hall at the
Viipuri City Library,
1930–1935

Walter Dorwin Teague,
interior of the Ford
Pavilion at the New York
World Exhibition, 1939

MODERNE

The French term Moderne refers to a form of **Art Deco** that was stylistically influenced by the **Modern Movement**. Although the Moderne style became popular in Europe during the 1920s and 1930s, it was in the United States that it really flourished. During this period, American promoters of the style, such as Walter Dorwin Teague and Raymond Loewy, used **streamlining** and gleaming **chromium** and **aluminium** surface finishes on their product designs to give them an alluring modernistic appearance. The luxurious Moderne style was also frequently distinguished by heavy geometric forms that were inspired by the **Wiener Werkstätte**. The sumptuous interiors and furniture designed by Donald Deskey exemplified the style and were mostly commissioned by corporate and wealthy private clients. Deskey's interior and furnishings for the Radio City Music Hall (1932–1933) also reflected the Moderne style's association with silverscreen glamour. But more than anything else, it was the extravagant glass and chrome sets of Hollywood films that internationally popularized the Moderne style. The opulence and inherent optimism of the style offered an illusory respite from the ravages of the Great Depression and came to symbolize the American Dream. The enormous impact of Moderne in the United States was responsible for many of the differences that still exist between American and European automotive and product **styling**. Many of the decorative aspects of the style were revived through **Post-Modernism** and late 20th-century **Retro Design**.

ORGANIC DESIGN

Ross Lovegrove,
Pod hanging lamp
for Luceplan,
1996–1997

Organic Design is a holistic and humanizing approach to design that was first pioneered in architecture in the late 19th century by Charles Rennie Mackintosh and Frank Lloyd Wright. Their method of working involved developing totally integrated **Gesamtkunstwerk** solutions whereby the whole of an architectural scheme was brought together in such a way that the complete effect was greater than the sum of its parts. Thus it was hoped that the whole work would capture something of the spirit of nature. Crucial to this organic approach was the consideration of how individual elements, such as objects and furniture, connected visually and functionally with the context of their interior setting and the building as a whole. Equally critical was how interiors connected visually and functionally with the whole of the scheme and how the building itself connected with its surrounding environment through the harmony of its proportions, use of materials and colour. While the interconnectedness and spirit of nature was at the heart of organic architecture, the use of organic forms was rare. It was not until the late 1920s and early 1930s that Alvar Aalto, one of the greatest advocates of Organic Design, pi-

Alvar Aalto, *Model
No. 43* chaise longue
for Artek, 1936

Charles & Ray Eames, *La Chaise* designed for the Museum of Modern Art's "International Competition for Low-Cost Furniture Design", 1948 (reissued by Vitra)

oneered a humanizing and modern organic vocabulary of form. The soft flowing curves of his revolutionary moulded plywood and laminated wood seat furniture countered the rigid geometric formalism of the **International Style**. Like earlier organic architecture, Aalto's designs were holistically conceived but his core concern was not so much with spiritual transcendence as with the functional, intellectual and emotional connections his furniture made with individual users. He believed that wood was "the form-inspiring, deeply human material" and rejected alienating industrial materials such as **tubular metal**, then the materials of choice of the European **avant-garde**. So widespread was the success of Aalto's furniture and the dissemination of his ideas, particularly in the United States, that he virtually single-handedly changed the course of design towards organic Modernism. In 1940, Eliot Fette Noyes organized the landmark competition "Organic Design in Home Furnishings" held at the Museum of Modern Art, New York, to promote this new and more mindful approach to design. In the accompanying catalogue, Noyes defined Organic Design as "an harmonious organization of the parts within the whole, according to structure, material, and purpose. Within this definition there can be no vain ornamentation or superfluity, but the part of beauty is none the less great – in ideal choice of material, in visual refinement, and in the rational elegance of things intended for use." [*Organic Design in Home Furnishings* catalogue, Museum of Modern Art, New York,

1941] The prize-winning entries for the "Seating for a Living Room" category, jointly submitted by Eero Saarinen and Charles Eames, were among the most important furniture designs of the 20th century. Their armchairs were revolutionary not only in the state-of-the-art technology they deployed in the construction of the chairs' single-form compound-moulded plywood seat shells but also for the concept of continuous contact and support advanced through the shells' ergonomically refined organic forms. These immensely influential designs heralded a totally new direction in furniture – encouraging attempts to achieve the ideal of structural, material and functional organic unity of design – and led directly to such seminal designs as Charles and Ray Eames' moulded **plywood** chairs (1945–1946) the amorphous *La Chaise* prototype (1948) and *Plastic Shell* series of chairs (1948–1950) as well as Eero Saarinen's *Womb* chair (1947–1948) and *Pedestal Group* of chairs and tables (1955–1956). The practical application of Organic Design also had a significant impact on Saarinen's architecture during the 1950s and in particular on his masterwork, the remarkably organic TWA Terminal (1956–1962) at Kennedy Airport – one of the most extraordinary buildings of the 20th century. While the success of Organic Design during the post-war years stylistically influenced the rise of **Biomorphism** in mainstream design, it continued to inspire designers working in the 1960s and the 1970s, such as

Maurice Calka,
Boomerang desk for
Leleu-Deshays, 1970

Ross Lovegrove, *Surf Collection* computer accessories for Knoll International, 1992

Maurice Calka, Pierre Paulin and Olivier Mourgue, to create highly sculptural forms in the organic idiom. By the early 1990s, fuelled by better ergonomic/ anthropometric data and by advances in **Computer-Aided Design and Manufacture**, **Organic Design** re-emerged stronger than ever. Like Eames and Saarinen before them, industrial designers at the cutting-edge today, such as Ross Lovegrove, seek to evolve essentialist organic designs through innovative applications of state-of-the-art materials and industrial techniques. While Organic Design is often associated with natural materials, it is, ironically, **plastics** – the ultimate in synthetic materials – that are best suited to expressing the abstract essence of nature and to maximizing functional connections by achieving the organic forms that most closely conform to our human morphology. Organic Design is at its most powerful, however, when its sensual and emotionally persuasive formal vocabulary connects with us subliminally by appealing directly to our primeval sense of natural beauty.

PACKAGING

Apothecary jars, 19th
century

Günter Kupetz, mineral water bottle,
1969 – this classic German design
(like the British milk bottle) has been
effectively recycled over a number
of decades and is used not only for
mineral water but also orangeade
and lemonade. It received a Gute
Form design prize in 1973.

Since the earliest commercial ventures, packaging has
been used as a means of preparing goods for efficient
transport, storage and sale. In the second half of the
19th century, however, the importance of packaging
increased dramatically when it began to be used by
Western manufacturers as a means of **branding** their
products. During this period, glass and ceramic jars,
pots, bottles and metal tins were emblazoned with
either moulded or transfer-printed names and logos,
together with claims that often exaggerated the properties of the products they contained. As packaging
became more sophisticated in the early 20th century,
many companies started commissioning leading
graphic designers to produce eye-catching designs,
often as part of a larger overall **corporate identity** programme. Lucian Bernhard's brightly coloured packaging for Bosch spark plugs, and Alfred Runge & Eduard
Scotland's bold graphics for Kaffee Hag coffee tins, for
example, helped the respective companies to powerfully
differentiate their products and achieve much brand
recognition. Since the onset of modern industrial food
production and mass retailing, packaging has become
increasingly necessary to protect goods from the hazards
of handling and environmental conditions, to provide
a convenient unit of the product for the manufacturer,
distributor and consumer, and to identify the product in
an appealing way to the consumer. Packaging today also
needs to be easy to manufacture and inexpensive rela-
tive to the cost of the final packaged product, to be
clearly tamperproof, and to comply with environmental
standards. As consumers have become more brand
conscious, the graphic design of packaging has become
evermore systemized, with particular graphic styles
being used to promote the idea of product families.

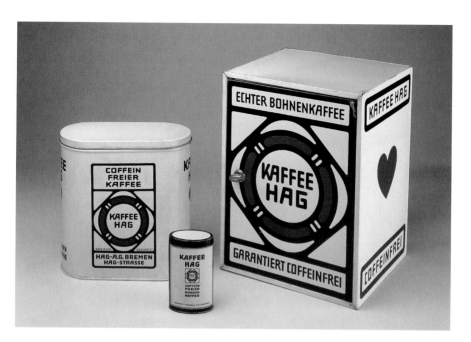

**Alfred Runge &
Eduard Scotland,**
Kaffee Hag coffee
tins, c. 1910

A notable example of this is Lewis Moberley's design of packaging for Boots
the Chemist. The graphic clarity of this completely integrated programme
gave items as diverse as low-calorie foodstuffs and laundry care products
a strong visual coherence and brand identity. Now that supermarkets stock
a greater selection of products every year and competition between brands
is more closely fought, "on-shelf impact" has become an essential packaging criterion. Colour, typography and branding are just some of the tools
used to grab consumers' attention when shopping. More important than
what is printed on the packaging is, however, the actual design of the container. Food packaging in particular must be designed to retard spoilage
and prevent physical damage and exposure to the elements. Especially critical is the design of closures, which must adequately seal the container in a
sanitary and mechanically safe way. One of the greatest pioneers in this field
of packaging was Dr. Ruben Rausing, who established Tetra Pak in 1951. He
believed that packaging should use a minimal amount of material while
providing the greatest degree of hygiene. This he achieved by developing a
tetrahedron-shaped carton made of polyethylene-coated paperboard. During
the 1950s and 1960s, **plastics** became widely available and began replacing
ceramics and glass as packaging materials. Since then, a variety of plastics
have been used in packaging applications, including polystyrene (PS), poly-

Lewis Moberley, packaging design for Boots Laundry range, c. 1995

propylene (PP), low density polyethylene (LDPE), polyvinyl chloride (PVC), high density polyethylene (HDPE), and polyethylene terephthalate (PET). Owing to their high durability, light weight, flexibility and insulation qualities, plastics are used extensively for packaging liquids, perishable foodstuffs, pressurized packages and containers of food intended to be frozen or boiled. Despite their many uses, plastics only account for about 14% (by volume) of all packaging in municipal solid waste streams. By far the greatest component, at approximately 50%, is cardboard (paper) – the most widely used consumer packaging material. Light in weight, inexpensive, easily manufactured, printed and sorted, cardboard cartons can be produced in a wide range of shapes and sizes, half of which are used for food packaging. Metallic containers, including tin-plated steel and **aluminium**, account for roughly 16% of all packaging and are also used primarily for food storage. Being highly resistant to chemical and mechanical damage, tin-plate containers are also used to hold chemical agents such as paints, preservatives and solvents, as well as aerosol products. Lighter and more malleable, aluminium is principally used in packaging for bottle caps and vacuum-sealed easy-open beverage cans. Glass containers, which are easily mass-produced and can be reused, make up approximately 20% of the packaging content of

Pethick & Money,
Flexible Food Wrap
fast-food packaging,
1996 – winner of two
BBC Design Awards,
this packaging
offers a significant
reduction of waste

municipal solid waste streams. Glass is chemical-resistant, durable and can be kept highly hygienic and is thus ideal for the packaging of solid and liquid food, cosmetics and drugs. While packaging is essential for the promotion and protection of merchandise, it tends to be used excessively by manufacturers, who regard it as a relatively inexpensive way of "adding value" to their products. In Europe today, packaging generally accounts for 25–35 % of the waste (by weight) in municipal solid waste streams. Despite growing concern about its impact on the environment, no real solutions to the problem of reducing packaging waste have been developed. Government-backed initiatives are inevitable, however, and will no doubt focus on programmes of waste prevention that balance recycling, reuse and a reduction of packaging materials. Light-weighting or down-gauging packaging to a safe minimum, as demonstrated by the *Flexible Food Wrap* designed by Pethick & Money for use in fast-food restaurants, is an essential component in waste prevention. Consumers, designers, manufacturers and governments will have to fundamentally and radically rethink the nature of packaging if waste is to be minimized and natural resources preserved.

BIC disposable
lighter, 1990s

PLANNED OBSOLESCENCE

Planned obsolescence is a highly contentious issue that lies at the heart of some of the most important debates on consumerism, global sustainability and **industrial design**. Having first emerged as a major feature of the American economy in the 1950s, planned obsolescence is based on the concept of intentionally limiting the life of products so that consumers are manipulated into consuming more – an approach that continues to form a key part of the strategies of many large manufacturing companies. There are two strongly conflicting views on the morality of planned obsolescence. Advocates claim that it keeps workers (and designers) in employment, is essential to economic growth and is ultimately beneficial to society as a whole. Opponents of planned obsolescence claim that the manipulation of consumers is insidious, that the value for money offered by limited-life products, no matter what the economics, is poor, and that the waste created by their premature replacement is environmentally ruinous. An early and notable opponent of planned obsolescence was Vance Packard, who wrote the seminal book *The Waste Makers* (1960), in which he identified the three principal spheres of obsolescence – function, quality and desirability. Functional obsolescence arises when a new product appears that is perceived to do a better job than its predecessors. The obsolescence of quality, which is directly related to the physical durability of a product, has historically been achieved by manufacturers building in

BIC disposable
razors, 1990s

to products key components that have been designed to fail after a given

amount of time. White goods, or domestic appliances, are particularly prone to this type of "built-in obsolescence", with, in most cases, the replacement of the entire unit being more cost-effective than the replacement of the defective component(s). The obsolescence of desirability operates mainly through changes in the appearance of products, fashion and consumer opinion, all of which are driven by **styling** and/or advertising strategies. As early as the 1920s, the chairman of General Motors, Alfred Sloan, recognized that aesthetics would play an increasingly important role in the automotive market and instigated a system of annual

Chevrolet *Impala* convertible, 1959 – the car as fashion accessory in *Vogue* magazine

stylistic changes so as to minimize the aesthetic durability of cars. While this approach is still common among many automobile manufacturers, those in Germany and Scandinavia have historically added much value to their brands and enjoyed increasing success and brand loyalty by raising the overall durability of their products. Thus annual sales of used Volvo cars actually surpass the number of new vehicles it produces each year (around 400,000). The huge and ever increasing secondary market for its vehicles and branded parts is massively profitable for the company. In the case of Volvo, durability equals profitability. While there are clearly good economic arguments against the supposed social benefits of planned obsolescence, the environmental argument is even more compelling, especially given the urgency of the need to take meaningful steps towards achieving global sustainability. Making products more durable reduces the throughput of energy and materials, lowers consumption of finite resources, cuts emissions of pollutants (including greenhouse gases) and produces less residual waste. By doubling the life span of products, their net environmental impact can be halved. Making-less-last-longer is not only good for the environment, it also maximizes value for money and convenience for the consumer. Taken to an extreme, planned obsolescence results in disposable products – the most wasteful and least environmentally justifiable of all consumer product types.

PLASTICS

Napkin rings cast
from phenolic resin,
late 1930s

Synthetic plastics quite literally moulded the material culture of the 20th century. So profound was their effect on mass consumerism that the period could be described as "The Plastics Age". As early as the 15th century, however, natural plastics such as shellac (the resin from a tropical beetle), casein (produced from milk curds) and keratin (a protein found in hair, fur, bone, nails, hoofs and horn) were being used in the manufacture of luxury goods. The development of the first modern plastic is generally credited to the English chemist and inventor, Alexander Parkes. During the 1840s, he discovered that wood-dust or cotton fibre, when dissolved in nitric acid or sulphuric acid and then combined with castor oil and chloroform, produced a dough-like substance that when dried looked remarkably like ivory or horn. This form of cellulose nitrate, scientifically known as pyroxylin, was difficult to work with because of its explosive nature and its inherent brittleness. Parkes subsequently set up a company to manufacture this semi-synthetic plastic, which he named Parkesine, but it went into receivership in 1868. In America, John Wesley Hyatt continued to search for something better than Parkesine which he could use as a synthetic alternative to ivory to make billiard balls. By mixing camphor under pressure with cellulose nitrate, he was able to solve the problem of brittleness and in 1869 he patented the first practical semi-synthetic plastic under the name of Celluloid. During the 1870s and 1880s Celluloid was used in the manufacture of all kinds of objects, including hair combs, brushes, buttons, hand mirrors, letter openers and dice. It could also be made to imitate ivory, tortoiseshell, mother-of-pearl and amber. Although significantly cheaper than these luxury materials, Celluloid was still relatively expensive and consequently did not suffer from the associations of cheapness that dogged successive synthetic materials. In 1889 George Eastman's firm (later renamed the Eastman Kodak Co.) marketed the first commercial transparent, flexible camera film made of Celluloid. From 1904, the Belgian-trained chemist and entrepreneur Leo Baekeland worked on the development of the first completely synthetic plastic and in 1907 perfected the manufacture of phenol-formaldehyde resin (also known as phenolic resin). Better known under its trade name **Bakelite**, this revolutionary material was produced commercially from 1910 and was marketed as "the material of a thousand uses".

Phenolic resin was initially used as a coating material, especially for metals, and as an adhesive, before being employed as a moulding powder. It was remarkably suited to moulding processes and from the 1920s onwards considerably changed the aesthetic of many industrially-manufactured products. In 1928 a method was perfected for "casting" phenolic resins without the need of a filler, such as had previously been required for the production of Bakelite and other synthetic thermoset plastics (i. e. plastics that solidify on heating and cannot be remelted or reformed without decomposing). It was now possible to cast phenolic resins in a wide range of bright colours. These strong, non-flammable and colourful materials were used for numerous articles including napkin rings and jewellery. Urea-formaldehyde thermoset resins were widely used from the late 1920s, including a product marketed under the trade name of Plaskon. With the development of melamine-formaldehyde in the late 1930s, urea-based plastic laminates gave way to Formica laminates. Then, as the demand for better-performing synthetic materials grew, so another major group of plastics began to emerge. These were the thermoplastics – plastics that soften when heated and can be moulded and remoulded repeatedly without any appreciable change in properties. Amongst the earliest of these was polyvinyl chloride (PVC), which was first manufactured as Vinylite by the Carbide & Carbon Chemical Corporation in 1928. Today, PVC is available in two forms, rigid (unplasticized) or flexible (plasticized) – the latter being used extensively for **packaging**. A polymer of PVC marketed under the trade name of Saran can be found in kitchen cling-films, for example. By the end of the Second World War, the range of thermoplastics had expanded to include polyethylene (PE), the most widely used plastic today, polystyrene (PS) and polymethyl methacrylate (PMMA), which is better known under its trade name Perspex. These were followed in the post-war years by polyurethane (PU), polypropy-

◤ Salt and pepper shakers for BEF Products, England, 1935 – produced using ureum

Chad Valley train-set for Chad Valley, England, 1940s – produced using Bakelite

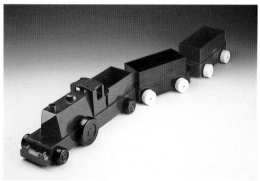

lene (PP), acrylonitrile-butadiene-styrene (ABS) and polyethylene terephthal-ate (PET). Each of these widely used commodity plastics has its own unique set of properties and is better suited to certain processes and applications than to others. Thus PET, for example, is best used for pressurized beverage containers that are blow-moulded. Plastics can also be reinforced with glass fibres to produce glass-fibre-reinforced plastic (GRP), more commonly known as Fibreglass. Combined with resins such as epoxies or unsaturated polyesters, thermoset glass-fibre reinforced plastic is pound-for-pound stronger than steel and has a wide range of applications, from furniture to car bodies. Today, an extensive array of plastics processing techniques are available to industrial designers and manufacturers, including extrusion (for the manufacture of films, sheets, tubing etc. in which the melted material is pushed through the orifice of a die); compression moulding (in which plastic pellets are heated and compressed into a mould at the same time); injection moulding (in which a molten resin is shot into a mould under considerable pressure, sometimes using nitrogen gas); reaction injection moulding (using a catalyst to speed up the reaction between two polyurethane precursors so that the moulding process requires less pressure); blow moulding (a molten polymer is blown into a mould to create a hollow moulding, e. g. plastic bottles); casting and dipping (inexpensive processes for the produc-

Erik Magnussen, salad bowls and salad servers for Stelton, 1986 – moulded PMMA (also known as Perspex)

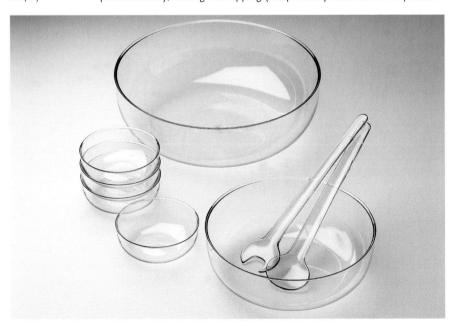

tion of small objects that require no pressure); rotational moulding (a low-heat, low-pressure process in which a mould is rotated so that the plastic fuses to the interior of the mould to produce hollow objects such as refuse bins); thermoforming (in which a heated sheet of thermoplastic such as polystyrene or PET is pulled by a vacuum into a mould, e. g., for drinking cups); and foaming (in which polystyrene is combined with isopentane to produce a material with gas bubbles that can be moulded or extruded, e. g. for egg cartons and fast-food packaging). Today, plastics account for approximately 14 % (by volume) of municipal solid waste, with most of that figure representing packaging. In order to allow more efficient material identification, sorting and ultimately recycling, many plastic objects, especially plastic packaging, now bear the international plastics coding system. Thanks to their easy manipulation, economical production, corrosion resistance and suitability to industrial processes, plastics remain among the most popular and useful materials. The highly innovative treatment of various advanced techno-polymers by some of today's most talented industrial designers has led recently to a significant reappraisal of the aesthetic of plastics in general.

⬉ **Stefano Giovannoni**, *Merdolino* toilet brushes for Alessi, 1993 – moulded technopolymer

Guido Venturini, *Gino Zucchino* sugar shakers for Alessi, 1993 – moulded PMMA

PLYWOOD

Alvar Aalto, group of plywood and laminated-wood furniture for Artek, on display at Bowman Brothers in London, c. 1938

Plywood and laminated wood have been used in furniture-making since the first half of the 18th century, and possibly even earlier. It was not until the late 1920s, however, that technological innovations in the production of modern wood laminates, and in particular the development of synthetic resin adhesives such as phenol- and urea-formaldehyde, enabled designers such as Alvar Aalto to begin fully exploiting the technical, formal and aesthetic potential of these materials. So successful was the application of plywood and laminated wood in furniture design that by the mid-1930s they had replaced **tubular metal** as the materials of choice for most **avant-garde** designers. Plywood is manufactured in panel form by gluing one or more layers of veneer to both sides of a single sheet of veneer or a core of solid or reconstituted wood. Each layer is typic-

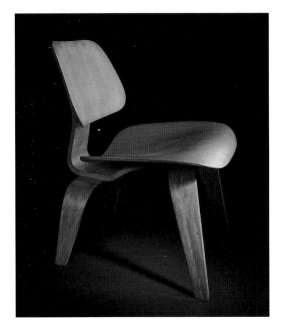

ally glued with its grain running at right angles to that of the layer above and/or below it, with each layer and grain direction being mirrored on the opposite side of the core. The total number of layers is almost always odd – three, five or more. Wherever there is a requirement to cover a large surface area with a lightweight but strong material, plywood may be used. Plywood has many advantages over solid wood, most importantly its increased dimensional stability and suitability for moulding into curved forms. Some of the largest applications of moulded plywood include aircraft, boat and furniture construction. Moulded plywood is produced by bending and glueing ven-

Gerald Summers, armchair for Makers of Simple Furniture, 1933–1934

←**Charles & Ray Eames**, *LCW* (Lounge Chair Wood) for Evans Products and later Herman Miller, 1945 – bent laminated wood frame with compound-moulded plywood seat and back

eer sheets in a combined operation, employing forms in conjunction with either cold press systems, hot press systems, bag or blanket press systems or radio frequency forming systems. Plywood is most easily moulded into one or more curves on one geometric plane, but can also be moulded into compound or complex curves on two geometric planes simultaneously. Either way, the radius of moulded plywood is normally limited by the thickness of the individual veneers and the construction and thickness of the plywood. The deformation capacity of moulded plywood is almost unlimited – a rule of thumb is that what can be formed with a sheet of paper (i. e. modelled) without deformation can be produced as a moulded plywood element. In making laminated wood, the veneers are glued so that their grains all run parallel to each other. Curved laminated wood is produced by bending and gluing at the same time. Unlike plywood, however, laminated wood can only be bent on one geometric plane (in the direction of the grain). Laminated wood again possesses several advantages over solid wood: it can be used for large elements of various sizes and shapes that would be impossible in solid wood, and it enables structures to be designed on the basis of required strength – the more veneers there are in either a plywood or laminated wood construction, the less likely critical failure becomes. Laminated wood is primarily used for structural applications, including architectural elements, boat keels and furniture components such as chair arms, legs and frames. Plywood and laminated wood are often used in combination, as famously demonstrated by the revolutionary range of chairs designed in 1945 by Charles & Ray Eames. These chairs were among the first examples of production furniture to incorporate compound-moulded seat elements, which provided a high degree of comfort without the need for traditional upholstery. The durability, strength, lightness, versatility, low cost, aesthetic appeal and suitability for industrial production of plywood and laminated wood has ensured that these materials remain an enduringly attractive option to furniture manufacturers and designers today.

POP DESIGN

Nivico 3240 GM television for JVC, (Yokohama Plant Victor Co. of Japan), 1970

The term Pop was coined in the 1950s and referred to the emergence of popular culture during that decade. In 1952, the **Independent Group** was founded in London and its members, including the artist Richard Hamilton, the sculptor Eduardo Paolozzi, the design critic Reyner Banham and the architects, Peter and Alison Smithson, were among the first to explore and celebrate the growth of popular consumer culture in America. In the 1960s, American artists too, such as Andy Warhol, Roy Lichtenstein and Claes Oldenburg began drawing inspiration from the "low art" aspects of contemporary life such as advertising, **packaging**, comics and television. Not surprisingly, Pop also began to manifest itself in the design of objects for everyday use, as designers sought a more youth-based and less serious approach than had been offered by the **Good Design** of the 1950s. The ascendancy of product **styling** in the 1950s, in the name of productivity-increasing **planned obsolescence**, provided fertile ground for the "use-it-today, sling-it-tomorrow" ethos that permeated industrial production during the 1960s. Peter Murdoch's polka-dotted cardboard *Spotty* child's chair (1963) and De Pas, D'Urbino and Lomazzi's PVC *Blow* chair (1967) were eminently disposable and epitomized the widespread culture of ephemerality. So too did the plethora of short-lived gimmicks such as paper dresses, which were lauded for their novelty in the large number of colour supplements and glossy magazines that became increasingly dependent on featuring such items. For many designers working within the Pop idiom, **plastics** became their materials of choice. By the 1960s, many new types of plastics and aligned processes, such as injection-moulding, became available and relatively inexpensive to use. The bright rainbow colours and bold forms associated with Pop Design swept away the last vestiges of post-war austerity and reflected the widespread optimism of the 1960s, which was bolstered by unprecedented economic prosperity and sexual liberation. Since Pop Design was aimed at the youth-market, products had to be cheap and were therefore often of poor quality. The expendability of such products, however, became part of their appeal as they represented the antithesis of the "timeless" Modern classics that had been promoted in the 1950s. Pop

Design with its **Anti-Design** associations countered the **Modern Movement**'s sober dictum "Less is More" and led directly to the **Radical Design** of the 1970s. It drew inspiration from a wide range of sources – **Art Nouveau**, **Art Deco**, **Futurism**, **Surrealism**, Op Art, Psychedelia, Eastern Mysticism, **Kitsch** and the Space-Age – and was spurred on by the growth of the global mass-media. The oil crisis of the early 1970s, however, necessitated a more rational approach to design and Pop Design was replaced by the **Craft Revival** on the one hand and **High Tech** on the other. By questioning the precepts of Good Design, and thereby Modernism, the influence of Pop Design was far-reaching and laid some of the foundations on which **Post-Modernism** was to grow.

Gaetano Pesce, *Up Series* for C&B Italia, 1969

POST-INDUSTRIALISM

Post-Industrialism is a term that mainly refers to a post-modern approach
to design whereby designed objects are produced outside the industrial
mainstream. From the 1910s to the 1960s, the mass-production methods of
Fordism dominated the design and manufacture of products, but during the
late 1970s and 1980s, as Western economies became less reliant on manufacturing industry and more service-based, many designers began creating
"one-off" or limited edition designs. This type of work not only reflected the
post-industrial nature of the period but also allowed designers to explore their
individual creativity more freely, because it was no longer subject to the constraints of the industrial process. Designers such as Ron Arad and Tom Dixon
constructed "rough-and-ready" artefacts that were consciously distanced
from the precision of standardized industrially manufactured products.
Arad's *Concrete* Stereo (1984), for instance, opposed the "good forms" associated with audio-equipment produced by companies such as Bang & Olufsen
and communicated a post-modern design rhetoric full of ironic content. Post-
Industrialism heralded the notion of "usable artwork" and as such, gave rise
to a new area of design practice that was both experimental and poetic.

Ron Arad, *Concrete
Stereo* for One-Off,
1984

POST-MODERNISM

**Marco Ferreri &
Carlo Bellini**, *Eddy*
lamp for Luxo
Italiana, 1986

**Norbert Berghof,
Michael Landes &
Wolfgang Rang,**
Frankfurter FIII chair
for Draenert,
1985–1986

The ancestry of Post-Modernism can be traced to the 1960s and
the emergence of **Pop-** and **Anti-Design**. During that decade, the
status quo was disputed in all areas of life, including the field of
modern design. The first questioning of Modernism appeared
most notably in Jane Jacobs, *The Death and Life of Great American Cities*
(1961), which focused on the break up of social cohesion brought about in
cities by the **Modern Movement**'s utopian building and planning schemes
and Robert Venturi's *Complexity and Contradiction in Architecture* (1966),
which argued that modern architecture was fundamentally meaningless,
for it lacked the complexity and irony that enriched historical buildings. In
1972, Venturi, Denise Scott Brown and Steven Izenour published the seminal book *Learning from Las Vegas,* which lauded the cultural honesty of the
commercialism found in the signage and buildings of this desert city. That
same year, the translation of Roland Barthes' *Mythologies* (1957) into English
led to the widespread dissemination of his theories on **semiotics** – the study
of signs and symbols as a means of cultural communi-
cation. The understanding then was that if buildings
and objects were imbued with symbolism, viewers
and users would be more likely to relate to them on
a psychological level. The early proponents of Post-
Modernism argued that the Modern Movement's espousal of geometric abstraction, which denied ornament and thereby symbolism, rendered architecture
and design dehumanizing and ultimately alienating.
From the mid-1970s, American architects, such as
Michael Graves, began to introduce into their designs
decorative motifs that frequently made reference to
past decorative styles and were often ironic in content.
Designers aligned to Studio Alchimia, such as Alessandro Mendini and Ettore Sottsass, began producing
work within the Post-Modern idiom that made ironic
comments on Modernism through the application of
applied decoration. Later, **Memphis** produced monumental and colourful "Neo-Pop" designs that, when ex-

hibited for the first time in 1981, caused an international sensation. Memphis' output was influenced by an eclectic range of sources and intentionally mocked the notion of "good taste" through its use of boldly patterned plastic laminates and quirky forms. Significantly, Memphis helped to popularize Anti-Design and in so doing contributed significantly to the acceptance of Post-Modernism as an international style during the 1980s. Post-Modern designs embraced the cultural pluralism of contemporary global society and used a language of shared symbolism so as to transcend national boundaries. The forms and motifs found in such "symbolic objects" were not only drawn from past decorative styles, such as Classicism, **Art Deco**, **Constructivism** and **De Stijl** but at times also made reference to **Surrealism**, **Kitsch** and computer imagery. Among the most notable Post-Modern designers (apart from those already mentioned) were Mario Botta, Andrea Branzi, Michele de Lucchi, Nathalie du Pasquier, Hans Hollein, Arata Isozaki, Shiro Kuramata, Richard Meier, Aldo Rossi, Peter Shire, George Sowden, Matteo Thun and Masanori Umeda. Their bold designs for **ceramics**, textiles, jewellery, watches, silverware, furniture and lighting were produced on a limited-scale by companies such as Alessi, Artemide, Alias, Cassina, Formica, Cleto Munari, Poltronova, Sunar, Swid Powell and

Michael Graves,
Tea & Coffee Piazza
for Alessi, 1983

Draenert Studio. As Hans Hollein noted, Post-Modernism's rejection of the industrial process meant that products in this style were invariably "an affair of the élite", and as such represented capitalism's triumph over the social ideology that was the basis of the Modern Movement. The eclectic nature of Post-Modernism reflected not only the ascendancy of individualism but also the increasingly fragmented nature of society during the 1980s. The credit-fuelled boom of this decade allowed the anti-rationalism of the Post-Modern style to flourish and by the late 1980s, Post-Modernism had become even more stylistically diverse, encompassing Matt Black, **Deconstructivism** and **Post-Industrialism**. The global recession of the early 1990s, however, moti-

Aldo Rossi, *Il Conico*
kettle for Alessi,
1988

vated designers to seek less expressive and more rational approaches to design and the appeal of Post-Modernism began to wane. Although the bold statements of 1980s Anti-Design were replaced with the muted purity of 1990s minimalism, the influence of Post-Modernism endures in that its questioning of the Modern Movement has led to an important and ongoing reassessment of what is essential in design.

PRODUCT ARCHITECTURE

**Richard Hamilton &
Martin Goody**,
House of the Future
for Monsanto, 1957

The idea of buildings being designed as mass-producible consumer products has fascinated both architects and industrial designers for many decades. One of the first notable examples of this type of product architecture was developed by Walter Gropius and Konrad Wachsmann. Their *Packaged House* system of 1942 rested on the idea of mass-producing modular components for the construction of domestic buildings. Although the concept was patented, it was not a resounding commercial success, with only 200 units being sold before the manufacturing company was liquidated. Between 1944 and 1947 Richard Buckminster Fuller designed the **aluminium**-clad *Dymaxion Dwelling Machine* (also known as *Wichita House*). When the prototype of this prefabricated building was launched, the company that was specially set up to commercialize it received 38,000 orders. Fuller was not prepared to begin manufacturing the house, however, until its design had been completely perfected. As a result, the project was seriously delayed and eventually cancelled by its financial backers. Undeterred, in 1949 Fuller invented the *Geodesic Dome*, which must be considered the most successful example of product architecture to date. A friend and colleague of Fuller's, George Nelson, also began designing a product architecture system in 1951. His *Experimental House* was based on a building system made up of cubes

Matti Suuronen,
Futuro House, early
1970s

(measuring 12' x 12') with translucent plastic domes that could be linked together. Because of its modularity, the *Experimental House* offered a greater degree of flexibility than Fuller's earlier *Dymaxion Dwelling Machine*. Arthur Drexler, the then curator of the Museum of Modern Art, New York, described Nelson's elegant solution as "a product technically superior to its handcrafted competitors". In 1957 Richard Hamilton and Marvin Goody designed the Monsanto

House of the Future as an exhibit for Tomorrowland at Disneyland. The four identical plastic elements that made up each wing of this futuristic-looking house predicted the capsule-like product architecture of the Finnish architect Matti Suuronen from the early 1970s. As the journal *Design from Scandinavia* noted, Suuronen's *Futuro House* "took the dream of a plastic house from laboratory to standard production at a single leap ... Ignoring all conventional housing concepts, he has created a huge lozenge which is placed on a fundament of steel piping." Comprising a floor area of 50 m², the *Futuro House* was nevertheless light enough to be slung by helicopter to inaccessible sites. Suuronen's later *Venturo House*, developed for Oy Polykem in Helsinki, was also constructed of highly insu-

Ross Lovegrove,
Solar Seed, 1999 –
concept for a wholly
autonomous
nomadic structure

lated, glass-fibre-reinforced polyester elements that were similarly easy to transport. The concept of product architecture has more recently been explored by the London-based industrial designer, Ross Lovegrove. His *Solar Seed* proposal speculates on a wholly autonomous nomadic structure that uses a minimal amount of material. Like his highly innovative designs for garden lighting, the *Solar Seed* is also intended to be solar-powered and produced with state-of-the-art manufacturing techniques. While the industrial production of complete architectural structures has remained elusive, mobile forms of living space such as the famous Airstream trailer and the Volkswagen camper have become design icons of the 20th century. Given the widespread and increasing need for affordable, flexible and transportable housing, the future success of product architecture will no doubt depend less on technical issues of construction and manufacture than on problems associated with local building regulations, siting and land ownership.

RADICAL DESIGN

Coop Himmelb(l)au,
Vodöl chair for Vitra,
1989

Radical Design emerged in Italy during the late 1960s as a reaction to **Good Design**. While similar to **Anti-Design**, Radical Design was more theoretical, politicized and experimental, and attempted to alter the general perception of Modernism through utopian proposals and projections. The primary exponents of Radical Design were the design and architectural groups Superstudio (founded 1966, Florence), Archizoom (founded 1966, Florence), UFO (founded 1967, Florence), Gruppo Strum (founded 1963, Florence), Gruppo 9999 (founded 1967, Florence), Cavart (founded 1973, Padua) and Libidarch (founded 1971, Turin). These groups attacked notions of what constituted "good taste" and staged subversive happenings and installations that questioned the validity of **Rationalism**, advanced technology and, above all, consumerism. Radical architectural projections, such as Superstudio's *Il Monumento Continuo* (Continuous Monument) of 1969 and Archizoom's *Wind City* of 1969, speculated on the idea of "architecture as a political instrument", while radical designs such as UFO's *Doric Temple* (1972) and Archizoom's *Superonda* (1966) were

**Cesare Casati &
Emanuele Ponzio,**
Pillola lamps for
Ponteur, 1968

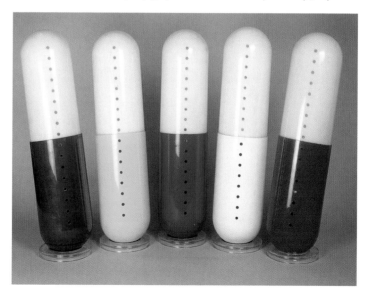

often characterized by their potential for user-interaction. At once poetic and irrational, designs such as these epitomized the counter-culture of the late 1960s and sought to destroy the hegemony of the visual language of Modernism. In 1973, members of the various Radical Design groups convened at the offices of *Casabella* magazine where Alessandro Mendini was director. The meeting led to the formation of Global Tools in 1974, but a year later this school of radical architecture and design was disbanded and the Radical Design debate briefly lost its impetus. By questioning long established precepts of the purpose of design, radical designers, such as Andrea Branzi, Riccardo Dalisi and Lapo Binazzi, laid the theoretical foundations from which **Post-Modernism** evolved in the late 1970s and early 1980s.

UFO Group (Lapo Binazzi), *Doric Temple* prototype, 1971

RATIONALISM

Giuseppe Terragni, conference room of the Casa del Fascio (later renamed Casa del Popolo) in Como, 1933

The term Rationalism refers in general to a logical approach to architecture and design but also denotes a form of Modernism pioneered by architects and designers in Italy during the late 1920s and 1930s. Inspired by both the social and aesthetic aspects of earlier modern work by architects such as Walter Gropius and Le Corbusier, the Gruppo Sette (Group of Seven) published a four-part manifesto in the magazine *Rassegna* in 1926 that effectively launched the Italian Rationalist movement. The group's members, which included Giuseppe Terragni, Gino Pollini, Luigi Figini, Adalberto Libera, Carlo Enrico Rava, Sebastiano Larco and Guido Frette, strongly opposed **Futurism** and instead sought to reconcile the **Functionalism** of the European **avant-garde** with Italy's Classical tradition. The first notable expressions of Italian Rationalism in architecture were Luciano Baldessari, Luigi Figini and Gino Pollini's Bar Craja in Milan (1930) and Giuseppe Terragni's Casa del Fascio in Como (1933). The Rationalists celebrated modern progress through a severe geometric formal vocabulary and the use of state-of-the-art materials such as chromed **tubular metal**. Rationalism was embraced by the Fascists, who regarded themselves as champions of a new world order, but eventually adopted the conservative Novecento style. After the Second World War, designers such as Franco Albini continued to perpetuate the Rationalist style.

RETRO DESIGN

Figaro car for
Nissan, 1991 –
produced as a
limited edition
of 20,000

Retro Design is a term that was first used in the mid-
1970s to describe a tendency in popular design to embrace previous historical styles. Throughout the 1960s and early 1970s there was a huge revival of
interest in Victoriana and **Art Nouveau**, with – for example – Victorian fair-
ground typography being used extensively for pop posters and album covers. Retro Design really came of age in the early 1980s, however, when **Post-
Modernism** became an international style. Many designers aligned with this
movement looked to the **Kitsch** products of the 1950s for inspiration, resulting in the emergence of a plethora of retro-designed products, including
radios in sickly pastel colours and asymmetrical furniture on spindly legs.
The allure of 1950s style continued well into the 1990s, with the *Figaro* car
launched as a limited edition by Nissan in 1991. This diminutive vehicle is
an almost cartoon-like representation of 1950s design, while the *Royal Star*
motorcycle designed by GK Design for Yahama is a more direct interpreta-
tion of the period style. More recently, Jaguar, BMW and Chrysler have also
produced blatantly retro-designed vehicles. Clearly a big business, Retro
Design today involves the combination of historicizing **styling** with up-to-
the-minute technology so as to produce hybrid products that function well
while projecting a strong sense of character.

GK Design Group,
Royal Star motor-
cycle for Yamaha,
1996

ROYAL COLLEGE OF ART

FOUNDED 1837
LONDON, GREAT BRITAIN

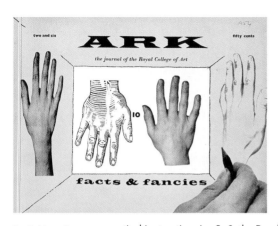

Len Deighton, Cover
for *Ark* journal, issue
10, Spring 1954

Founded as the Government School of Design in 1837, the college was initially concerned with the teaching of the "grammar of ornament" and drawing from nature was discouraged. The teaching structure devised by Sir Henry Cole focused primarily on the training of students as "ornamentalists" for the manufacturing industries. Although a department of practical art was set up in 1852, it was not until the 1890s that more emphasis was placed on practical instruction. In 1896, the Royal College of Art adopted its present name and a new programme of teaching was implemented, which included classes in history, philosophy and architectural drawing for all first year students. Following this preliminary course, students selected one of four specialized areas of study – decorative painting, sculpture, architecture or design. Design reforms that germinated at the Royal college in the 1890s were later propagated at the **Bauhaus** and thereby had a direct bearing on the evolution of the **Modern Movement**. Until the 1950s, however, craft training rather than design teaching permeated the curriculum. In 1959, the Design Research Department and School of **Industrial Design** were opened, heralding a new professionalism at the college, which since then has been at the forefront of design practice.

RUBBER

Hot-water bottle made by Haffenden Moulding Company, 1996

The elasticity, resilience and strength of rubber make it ideally suited to a wide range of applications, from vehicle components to electrical insulation. Natural rubber, a polymer of isoprene, is obtained from plants such as the *Hevea braziliensis* tree, which produces a latex containing around 35% rubber that is tapped from grooves specially cut into its bark. The milky latex is then strained of impurities and diluted with water before being coagulated into its solid form. Although natural rubber was first scientifically described by François Fresneau and Charles-Marie de la Condamine in 1735, its use was not fully exploited until the American inventor Charles Goodyear developed the vulcanization process in 1839. This method of treating rubber with sulphur under heat and pressure greatly improved the material's strength and elasticity. Vulcanized rubber found one of its first applications in the manufacture of car and bicycle tyres. Gutta-percha, which has the same elemental composition as natural rubber but a different molecular structure,

Gutta-percha *Ocobo* golf balls made by James B. Halley, c. 1920

Calculator produced by Marksmark Products, c. 1997 – combining advanced synthetic elastomer with plastic to give a greater degree of tactility

was also widely used in the 19th century. Considered a natural plastic, gutta-percha is a rubber-like substance that can be moulded easily when heated but which becomes hard and leathery at room temperature. Because of its good heat-resistance, natural rubber is still used today for high-performance tyres such as those used on racing cars and aircraft. During the late 19th and early 20th century, several attempts were made at producing synthetic rubber from isoprene. It was not until the First World War, however, that scientists in Germany successfully developed the first synthetic "methyl rubber" by polymerising butadiene. By the 1920s and 1930s synthetic rubber was being manufactured by several polymerisation methods and during the Second World War large amounts were produced from butadiene polymers. Like natural rubber, synthetic rubber can be vulcanized and reinforced with fillers and is especially suited to casting and compression-moulding processes. Over half the rubber currently produced is used for the manufacture of vehicle tyres, while the rest is used for the manufacture of mechanical components and consumer products, ranging from hot-water bottles and garden hoses to shoes and toys. Today, advanced synthetic elastomers are frequently used in conjunction with **plastics** for co-injecting moulding in order to give the casings of electronic products an enhanced tactile quality.

SECESSION

FOUNDED 1897
VIENNA, AUSTRIA

Josef Maria Olbrich, poster for the II Secessionist exhibition in Vienna, 1889 – showing Olbrich's Vienna Secession building

In 1897, the Vereinigung bildender Künstler Österreichs-Secession (Association of Austrian Artists) was founded by the artists Gustav Klimt, Carl Moll and Josef Engelhart and the architects Josef Maria Olbrich, Koloman Moser and Josef Hoffmann as a breakaway group opposed to the staid academic tradition of the conservative Künstlerhaus. In 1897, Olbrich designed his famous Secession Building with its large gilded dome of laurel leaves – a suitably imperial motif for Vienna. Completed in 1898, the building, situated on Karlsplatz, provided a permanent exhibition centre for the group. It has stained-glass panels and interiors designed by Moser and above its entrance an inscription by the art critic Ludwig Hevesi, which reads: "Der Zeit ihre Kunst, der Kunst ihre Freiheit" (To the age its art, to art its freedom), encapsulates the *fin-de-siècle* spirit of Vienna – by then the fourth largest city in Europe. Although it was not ready in time for the first Secession exhibition, which was held instead at the Horticultural Hall in Vienna, Olbrich's building was the venue for the second Wiener Sezession exhibition and subsequent displays of the group's work. To further promote their cause, the Secession also published their own journal, *Ver Sacrum* (Sacred Spring) from 1898. Though the Secession's early work was essentially within the **Art Nouveau** style, their output became increasingly rectilinear after the landmark VIII Wiener Sezession exhibition of 1900, which was dedicated solely to the decorative arts. This exhibition included installations by Charles Rennie Mackintosh, Charles Robert Ashbee and Henry van de Velde. Josef Hoffmann's Purkersdorf Sanatorium (1904–1906) with its unrelenting geometry, which was echoed in Koloman Moser's black and white cubic armchair designed specifically for the project, exemplified the post-1900 Secessionist style and anticipated the geometric abstraction of the **Modern Movement**. Inspired by Charles Ashbee's Guild of Handicraft, Hoffmann and Moser, together with the banker Fritz Waerndorfer, founded the **Wiener Werkstätte** in 1903 to produce and retail "New Art" designs by members of the Vienna Secession. There were, however, growing tensions within the Secession, and when in 1905 the artist Carl Moll was attacked by other members Klimt and his followers – known as the "stylists" –

left the group as did Hoffmann. The Secession nevertheless continued to operate, and from 1919 to 1920 Franz Messner was its president. Although often associated with Art Nouveau, the Vienna Secession was influenced by Classicism to a greater extent than other reforming artists' groups on the Continent. Its promotion of a geometric vocabulary of form had a profound impact on the evolution of Modern design.

SEMIOTICS

First introduced into philosophical debate by the 17th-century English politician and philosopher, John Locke, semiotics refers to the study of signs and symbols, which although most commonly applied to linguistics can be relevant to visual language. Throughout the history of design, buildings, interiors and objects have been decorated with symbols to convey meanings and values or to impart character. Many designers associated with the **Arts & Crafts Movement**, for example, such as Charles F. A. Voysey and Charles Rennie Mackintosh, produced designs as much for the mind as to fulfil functional needs and sought to infuse their work with spiritual meaning through the use of motifs such as pierced hearts, circles and squares, which symbolized love, the body and the spirit. The Swiss psychologist and psychiatrist, Carl Jung undertook much research into symbols, especially alchemic ones, which he believed to be codes of the unconscious. The study of semiotics (or semiology as it is sometimes called) was also taken up in the early 20th century by the Austrian-born English philosopher, Ludwig Wittgenstein, who evolved his "picture theory" in the 1920s, suggesting that signs are pictures of reality; by the Swiss linguist Ferdinand de Saussure who proposed that the language of signs is a social phenomenon, and by the American philosopher, Charles Sanders Peirce who argued that semiotics was a logical and "formal doctrine of signs". These analytical researches into semiotics did not so much attempt to reveal the meaning of signs as to expose their underlying bias – for example, towards gender, class or race. In 1938, the American behavioural semanticist, Charles Morris, divided semiotics into three branches of study: pragmatics (the way in which signs are used), semantics (the meaning of signs) and syntax (the arrangement of signs). Later, semiotics was seen as a tool with which to analyse the visual world and the Italian writer and semiotician, Umberto Eco, who published *A Theory of Semiotics* (1976) and *Semiotics and the Philosophy of Language* (1984), was the first to apply this area of study to architecture. Later, Roland Barthes contributed much to the debate surrounding semiotics with a series of literary works including his famous book *Mythologies* (1957), which was translated into English in 1972 and became highly influential to the evolution of **Anti-Design**. By the 1970s, it was widely believed that the **Modern Movement**'s aesthetic, founded on pure geometric abstraction, was ulti-

mately alienating, because its lack of ornament – signs and symbols –
denied a basic means of cultural communication. Post-Modernists, such
as Charles Jencks urged for a return to symbolism in architecture and design, and during the 1980s semiotics gained much ground through **Post-
Modernism**. Today, many designers regard visual communication as an
important aspect of design practice and seek to imbue their work with
meaning or character through the application of semiotic theory.

SIGNAGE

Design Research Unit, signage for the Festival of Britain, 1951

Like **packaging**, signage can be considered a discipline within the field of "industrial" graphics. Its design imperatives are thereby visual clarity and a logical and aesthetic coherence. Signage frequently forms the subset of a larger **corporate identity** or municipal design programme, such as that developed by Edward Johnston in 1916 for London Transport. In the 1930s, Continental Europe responded to the need for clearer signage on its increasingly busy roads with the formulation of protocols governing road signage design. Later, in the 1960s, the burgeoning of the motorways led the British government to commission the *Worboys Report* on road signage. The Ministry of Transport subsequently commissioned Jock Kinneir and Margaret Calvet to design a new road signage system for use in Great Britain. It is a tribute to the designers' skill that the resulting Motorway Signage System (1964) is still in use today. Many multi-disciplinary design consultancies have designed fully-integrated signage systems for public events, public buildings and local government, as in the case of the Festival of Britain (Design Research Unit, 1951), the Victoria and Albert Museum (Pentagram, 1988) and the City of Rome (Ninaber, Peters & Krouwel, 2000).

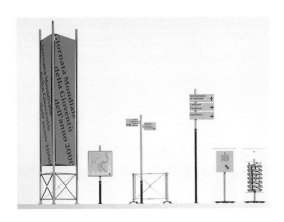

Ninaber, Peters & Krouwel (NPK), signage for the City of Rome, 2000

SOFT DESIGN/ SOFT-TECH

During the mid-1980s the term "soft-tech" was coined to describe products that used rounded or "softened" sculptural forms. One of the first manifestations of soft-tech was in consumer electronic equipment, most notably in products by Sharp and Yamaha. Post-modern designs like these opposed the pervasive **Rationalism** and "good forms" promoted by manufacturers such as Bang & Olufsen and were inspired instead by period styles, especially 1950s' **Biomorphism**. This type of American retro **styling** became a widespread phenomenon in the mid to late 1980s. It gave way in the early 1990s, however, to a more considered, organic and holistic approach to design. Described by Ross Lovegrove as "a new naturalism", soft design (as it became known) was emotional, gestural and human-centric. Remarkably, the car industry was amongst the first to embrace the new approach, as demonstrated by the Renault *Twingo* (1992) and the Nissan *Micra* (1992). The emergence of soft design can be attrib-

Frazer Designers, *Cobra* microscope for Vision Engineering, 1997

Fiat *Multipla*, 1999

George Sowden,
Dauphine desktop
calculator for Alessi,
1997

uted to a number of factors: the outright rejection, by the late 1980s, of **Bauhaus**-style **Functionalism** and the re-appraisal of **Organic Design** in general; the improved application of ergonomic data and the realization of more complex curved shapes made possible by advanced **Computer-Aided Design/-Manufacture** software; and the availability of new materials, especially exotic techno-polymers, offering products the potential for greater tactility. By the late 1990s soft forms had made significant in-roads not only into the car industry, as the Fiat *Multipla* (1999) shows, but also into mainstream design practice, and products ranging from microscopes and calculators to furniture and even MRI body scanners took on seductive sculptural forms. Soft design is often used stylistically and should not be confused with organic **essentialism**, which although bearing striking visual similarities is purely design-led.

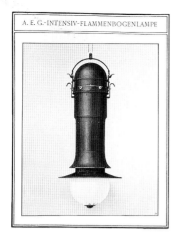

STANDARDIZATION

Peter Behrens, light fixture for AEG, 1908

Standardization is a crucial aspect of industrial mass production. The use of standardized components, which can be fitted together with little or no adjustment and interchanged from one product to another, increases efficiency and output. Early advocates of standardization included members of the **Deutscher Werkbund**, such as Hermann Muthesius, who saw it as a powerful tool for the democratization of design. One of the first companies to implement a coherent system of standardization was AEG, whose integrated product line, designed by Peter Behrens, reflected a deep understanding of Modern manufacturing techniques. The importance of standardization was again stressed at the Dessau **Bauhaus,** and associated designers such as Marcel Breuer, Gerhard Marcks and Wilhelm Wagenfeld produced standardized designs intended for large-scale industrial production. In France, Le Corbusier designed a standardized housing unit (1925) and a range of systemized furniture (1928) which included standardized modular storage units. The industrial designers of the post-war era fully embraced standardization, which offered the optimum means of manufacture and allowed the design of cost-effective product systems.

Charles and Ray Eames, *DAR (Dining Armchair Rod),* armchair for Zenith Plastics/Herman Miller Furniture Co., 1948–1950

Charles and Ray Eames' plastic shell group of chairs (1948–1950) and Robin Day's *Polyprop* series (1962–1963), for instance, both employed single standardized seat shells that could be attached to a variety of bases to create different options. Today, this standardized approach is common practice in all areas of design, from computer systems to **corporate identity** programmes.

Pages from Standard Möbel GmbH's "Das Neue Möbel" catalogue showing standardized furniture by Marcel Breuer, 1928

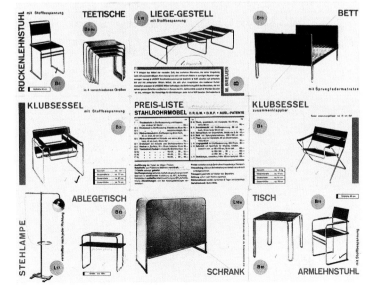

STREAMLINING

Streamlining involves the contouring of objects into rounded, smoothly finished and often teardrop-shaped aerodynamic forms so as to reduce their drag or resistance to motion through air. Streamlining was first used in the early 20th century to improve the performance of aircraft, locomotives and automobiles when moving at high speeds. By the 1930s, however, industrial designers were using streamlining less for functional reasons than to make household products look sleeker and thereby more appealing to the consumer. In America, the Wall Street Crash of 1929 and the ensuing Great Depression, together with the implementation of the price-fixing National Recovery Act of 1932, meant that manufacturers were operating within a fiercely competitive marketplace. Rather than investing in the development of entirely new products, many manufacturers preferred to re-style or "streamline" their existing products so as to make them appear new. Streamlining also helped manufacturers differentiate their products from those of their competitors, while annual restyling programmes – such as that implemented by Harley Earl at General Motors – became a deliberate means of accelerating the aesthetic obsolescence of products and thereby increasing sales. Interestingly, many of the American designers who became renowned for their streamlined designs,

Carl Breer, Chrysler *Airflow* (1934) with Union Pacific *City of Selina* locomotive (1934)

Ben Bowden, *Bicycle of the Future* (battery-operated) exhibited in "Design for the Future" section at the "Britain Can Make It" exhibition, 1946

such as Raymond Loewy, Norman Bel Geddes, Henry Dreyfuss and Walter Dorwin Teague, had previously worked as fashion illustrators, stage designers or commercial artists. Using clay models, such designers created sleek, modern-looking forms for a whole range of consumer goods, including refrigerators, vacuum cleaners, radios, cameras and telephones. Many of these products featured casings of **Bakelite**, a thermoset plastic eminently suited to the moulding of streamlined forms. In 1934 Loewy's *Coldspot* streamlined refrigerator for Sears became the first domestic appliance to be marketed on its looks rather than on its performance. The use of streamlining rapidly became widespread, and its practitioners highly celebrated. As Harold van Doren observed in 1940: "Streamlining has taken the world by storm ... The manufacturer who wants his laundry tubs, his typewriters, or his furnaces streamlined is in reality asking you to modernise them, to find the means for substituting curvilinear forms for rectilinear forms." In 1949 Raymond Loewy became the first designer to be featured on the front cover of *Time* magazine, his picture accompanied by the telling copy-line, "He streamlines the sales curve". By "adding value" to products at relatively little cost and stimulating sales, streamlining helped American manufacturing industries regain strength and profitability.

STYLING

Radio, mid-1950s

While design and styling are completely distinct disciplines, styling is often a complementary element of a
design solution. Styling is concerned with surface treatment and appearance – the expressive qualities of a product. In contrast,
design is primarily concerned with problem-solving – it tends to be holistic
in its scope and generally seeks simplification and essentiality in products.
Historically, styling has been used either to disguise the inherent mechanical aspect of a product, or to highlight it through the application of exaggerated symbolic forms. Raymond Loewy regarded stylistic "sheathing" as
a means of developing "the self-expression of the machine". Very often,
styling is used by manufacturers as a means of "adding value" to products
because it can dramatically enhance consumer appeal and increase product
differentiation. As Raymond Loewy insightfully noted: "Between two products equal in price, function, and quality, the better looking will outsell the
other." The prevalence of design over styling – or vice versa – is something
which has fluctuated over the course of the 20th century in line with the economic cycles of Western economies. Thus design (**Rationalism**) tends to
come to the fore during economic downturns, while styling (anti-rational-

KNR radio, mid-
1950s

ism) is apt to flourish in periods of economic prosperity. Styling found early expression in the 1920s, with the flourishing of **Art Deco**, and in the late 1930s and 1940s, when **streamlining** became a widespread phenomenon in American **industrial design**. The mid to late 1950s saw the emergence of biomorphic styling in opposition to the "good forms" perpetuated by the international design establishment through its well-established canons of "good taste", while the Pop-influenced products of the 1960s focused on short-lived stylistic gimmicks rather than on the long-lasting design solutions. With the rise of **Post-Modernism** in the applied arts in the 1980s, the transmission of meanings and values through aesthetics (i.e. surface treatment) became more important to the **avant-garde** than technical function. As well as being employed to make a product more attractive or symbolically meaningful, styling has also been used as a means of **planned obsolescence**. Having first emerged in the American automobile industry in the 1920s, stylistic planned obsolescence significantly accelerated product lifecycles. Annual re-styling programmes ensured that what was today the "latest thing" would be completely out of date within just a couple of years. This trend culminated most spectacularly in the decorative **chromium** flourishes of 1950s American automobile styling – and most worryingly in the actual compromising of vehicle safety for the sake of stylist devices. Although car manufacturers have toned down annual appearance changes in more recent years, styling continues to play an important role in the automotive industry, as evidenced by the prevalence of **Retro Design**. Today, styling is integrated into the whole of the design process and is applied from the beginning of a

Raymond Loewy, restyled Coca-Cola dispenser, 1940s – before (left) and after (right)

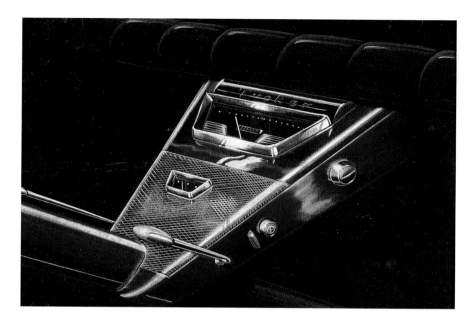

Preston Tucker and
Harry Miller, design
for a car dashboard
for Tucker of Chicago,
1946–1948

product's development rather than as an afterthought. In defining the differences between design and styling, the famous Italian industrial and furniture designer Vico Magistretti stated: "Design does not need drawing, but styling does. What I mean by this is that an object of design could be described … by spoken or written words, because what materializes through the process is a precise function, and, in particular, a special use of materials which, as a matter of principle, leaves all aesthetic questions out of consideration because the object is to achieve a precise practical aim. That does not of course mean that a precise image cannot be produced that will reflect and express 'aesthetic' qualities proper to the new methodology used in the conception of the object. Styling, on the other hand, has to be expressed by the most exact drawings, not because it disregards function but simply because it wraps that function in a cloak of essentially expressed qualities that are called 'style' and that are decisive in making the quality of the object recognizable."

SURREALISM

Surrealism was directly inspired by the researches into the subconscious and the analysis of dreams undertaken by Sigmund Freud. As an artistic movement, it can also be seen to have evolved from Symbolism and Dada, which it replaced. The poet, Guillaume Apollinaire is thought to have first coined the term in 1917, while the poet André Breton wrote the *Manifeste du Surréalisme* in 1924. In this publication, he defined Surrealism as "pure psychic automatism, by which it is intended to express ... the real process of thought. It is the dictation of thought, free from any control by the reason and of any aesthetic or moral pre-occupation." During the 1920s, proponents of Surrealism such as Salvador Dalí and Man Ray created assemblages that sought to combine objectivity with subjectivity, reason with nonsense and the conscious with the subconscious. During the 1930s, the Surrealist movement became increasingly politicized and many of its members became actively involved with the Communist Party. Its anti-rational stance countered pre-conceived notions of what art or design could be and blurred the distinctions between them – Salvador Dalí's *Mae West* sofa of c. 1936, for instance, can be considered a functional work of art.

Man Ray, *Le Témoin (The Witness)* chair for Gavina, 1971

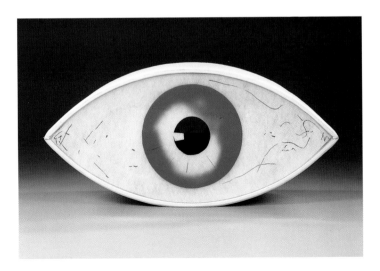

SWISS SCHOOL

auch Du bist liberal

Karl Gerstner, *auch Du bist liberal (You too are liberal)* poster, 1959

The term Swiss School refers to a typographic style developed in Zurich and Basel prior to and during the Second World War. As Switzerland remained politically neutral during the war, Swiss designers were able to develop the typographic theories that had been advanced earlier at the **Bauhaus**. Ernst Keller, who taught at the Kunstgewerbeschule in Zurich from 1918, had previously established a national reputation for typographic excellence and innovative graphic design. His student, Theo Ballmer, who trained at the Bauhaus, combined a rational approach with spatial principles inspired by **De Stijl** to create a grid system for layouts. The Swiss School's graphics of the 1920s were typified by the use of photomontage and new typefaces (ie. sans-serif typography). During the 1930s, Max Bill, who had also trained at the Bauhaus, introduced a form of asymmetrical layout to the Swiss School that was influenced by **Constructivism**. Sometimes referred to as the "International Graphic Style", in the 1930s and 1940s the Swiss School was characterized by the use of sans-serif type, "white space" and "objective photography" (i. e. realistic images). The resulting reductivist aesthetic was precise, direct and clinical. The Swiss School's graphics were displayed at the 1939 "Swiss National Exhibition", and during the 1950s its influence was spread internationally through the journal *New Graphic Design*, which was launched in 1959. The success of Swiss School typefaces, such as *Univers* 1954 designed by Adrian Frutiger and *Helvetica* redesigned in 1957 by Max Mieddinger, also contributed much to the Swiss School's international standing. During the 1960s, Karl Gerstner and Wolfgang Weingart began experimenting with more expressive compositions while continuing to follow the Modern approach of the Swiss School.

TAYLORISM

Early time and
motion study

Taylorism is a term used to describe an approach to
mass production that is based on an industrial management system pioneered by the mechanical engineer
Frederick Winslow Taylor. In 1881 Taylor developed and
implemented the concept of time studies, having realized that productivity could be enhanced if tasks per-
formed by workers were broken down into constituent parts and then scientifically analyzed so as to eliminate any waste of time or motion. His book,
The Principles of Scientific Management (1911), set forth his common-sense
principles not only for the organization of specific tasks but also for the
overall running of factories, and was highly influential upon Henry Ford,
amongst others. Taylor believed that his approach would bring "the elimination of almost all causes for dispute and disagreement" between employer
and employee. While Taylorism was initially regarded as dehumanizing, and
led to the greater implementation of automation, it resulted in the rise of a
new generation of highly skilled and empowered machine operators.

Still from Charlie
Chaplin's *Modern
Times*, a film reflect-
ing on the alienating
effect of the pro-
duction line

Cover of Mauser
catalogue, 1939

TUBULAR METAL

Tubular metal was first manufactured in Germany,
where Max and Reinhard Mannesmann patented processes used in its mass production in 1885. Five years
later Reinhard Mannesmann founded the Mannsmann-
röhren-Werke in Düsseldorf, which became the leading
producer of tubular metal. The Mannesmann process
involved the spinning of a solid rod of hot steel between
two inclined rollers that rotated in the same direction
so as to pull the rod over a mandrel bar (a spindle-like
element) to produce a tubular section. Unlike earlier piping, Mannesmann
tubular metal was seamless and consequently possessed greater strength
as well as better aesthetic qualities. Tubular metal found one of its first successful commercial applications in the construction of bicycles, including
models manufactured by the German company, Adler. At this stage, the
tubing used for bicycles had an outside diameter ranging from 95 mm to

**Ludwig Mies van
der Rohe,** *Model
No. MR20* armchair
for Berliner Metall-
gewerbe Joseph
Müller, 1927

THONET

THONET

380 mm. During the early years of the 20th century, tubular metal began to be used in the construction of other types of vehicles, as its strength, lightness and resilience made it a good substitute for wood. Furthermore, angled sections that were traditionally riveted could now be replaced with welded sections of tubing. The well-known Dutch aircraft designer and manufacturer Anthony Fokker used welded tubular metal in the construction of his first plane, the *Spin Mark I* (1910). Subsequent models of his aeroplanes produced in Germany during the First World War also incorporated tubular metal in their construction. Portable welding equipment developed at that time made tubular metal designs even more adaptable. In the early 1920s both Maschinenfabrik Sack GmbH and Josef Gassen were granted patents relating to manufacturing processes that produced improved tubular metal with thinner walls. In 1925 Marcel Breuer became the first designer to use tubular metal in the construction of furniture. His famous *Model No. B3 Wassily* chair (1925–1927) powerfully exploited the machine aesthetic of tubular metal as well as its inherent material qualities. A year later, the Dutch architect Mart Stam constructed a cantilevered prototype chair made of rigid gas pipes welded together, which inspired later tubular-metal designs, most notably by Marcel Breuer and Ludwig Mies van der Rohe, that were nickel-plated or **chromium**-plated. During the late 1920s and 1930 several manufacturers became renowned for their Modernist tubular-metal furniture, including Gebrüder Thonet, Standard-Möbel and PEL. Tubular metal also became a material of choice for **Moderne** designers of the 1930s, who exploited its gleaming aesthetic for stylistic purposes. Until the widespread availability of **plastics** in the 1950s and 60s, tubular metal was used extensively for contract furnishings. Today it continues to be used for a plethora of applications, ranging from motorcycle frames to golf-club shafts.

UTILITARIAN DESIGN

CATALOGUE PRICE One Shilling.

Cover of the first
Utility Furniture
catalogue, 1943

→ James Leonard,
stacking aluminium
and plywood school
chairs, 1948

Aynsley China coffee
cup and saucer, 1956

Utilitarian design is based on the concept that the primary criterion of virtue is utility. For centuries many different types of artefacts – from agricultural tools to cookware – have been designed purely for use rather than beauty. But in fulfilling technical practical requirements as logically, efficiently and inexpensively as possible, it has long been recognized that utilitarian designs, whether handcrafted or machine produced, project a distinct aesthetic or kind of beauty based on functional purity. The honesty and fitness for purpose that is characteristic of utilitarian design became the basis of the **Modern Movement**'s dictum, "form follows function". During the 1920s and 1930s, Modernists such as the Dutch architect Jacobus Johannes Pieter Oud produced utilitarian furniture purged of all ornament. Designs like these were strongly inspired by the socialist ethos of the Modern Movement. It was argued that the more rational a design, the cheaper its manufactured cost would be and hence the more accessible it would be to the working classes. This approach to the design of consumer products, however, did not take into account the conservative taste that permeated that sector of society at which the designs were primarily aimed. The most notable large-scale programme of utilitarian design was implemented in Britain between 1941 and 1951, when government-approved Utility furniture and textiles were made available to the British public in an effort to boost the domestic manufacturing economy at a time when many materials were still rationed. In recent years, **avant-garde** designers such as Jasper Morrison have begun producing essentialist product designs which project an aesthetic that is again very much utilitarian in nature.

VKHUTEMAS

FOUNDED 1920
MOSCOW, RUSSIA

Alexander Rodchenko, furnishing for the workers' club reading-room for the Russian pavilion at the 1925 Paris "Exposition des Arts Décoratifs"

The Vkhutemas (Higher State Artistic and Technical Workshops) evolved from the earlier Svomas (Free State Art Studios), founded in 1918. This progressive Soviet design workshop-cum-school numbered many leading Constructivists among its instructors, including Alexander Rodchenko, Varvara Stepanova, Vladimir Tatlin, Naum Gabo, Antoine Pevsner, Liubov Popova and Alexander Vesnin. The institution promoted the concept of "production art" and established contacts with industry. It also developed progressive teaching techniques and had close links with the **Bauhaus** through El Lissitzky, Kasimir Malevich and Wassily Kandinsky. Like other Soviet art institutions, such as Inkhuk (Institute of Artistic Culture) and Izo (fine arts department of Narkompros), the Vkhutemas played a crucial role in forming artistic ideology in the Soviet Union. Although the Russian **avant-garde** were initially supported by the Bolshevik regime, they were eventually persecuted by the Soviet Central Committee. In 1932, all architectural and design organizations, including the Vhutein (Higher State Artistic and Technical Institute), which had replaced the Vkhutemas in 1927, were abolished in favour of Party controlled unions.

WIENER WERKSTÄTTE

1903–1932
VIENNA, AUSTRIA

The Wiener Werkstätte were officially founded in June 1903 in Vienna by the Secessionist designers Josef Hoffmann and Koloman Moser and the wealthy banker, Fritz Wärndorfer. The cooperative was based on pioneering British organizations, most notably Charles Ashbee's Guild of Handicraft and was similarly dedicated to the pursuit of artistic endeavour through craftsmanship. By October 1903, various workshops had been established for silver and goldsmithing, metalwork, bookbinding, leatherwork and cabinet-making as well as an architectural office (previously Hoffmann's) and a design studio. The Wiener Werkstätte were remarkable for their cleanliness, lightness and exemplary treatment of workers – workmen in the cabinet-making workshop, for instance, received a virtually unheard of one to two weeks' paid leave. The designs produced by the Werkstätte bore not only the monograms of the designers but also those of the craftsmen who executed them, reflecting the organization's endeavour to promote equality between artist and artisan. Its members, especially Hoffmann, refused to compromise quality for affordablity and insisted on using the best available materials. Although this approach ensured excellence, it also hindered financial success and meant that the Werkstätte's democratizing influence was not as widespread as it might have been. By 1905, however, the Wiener Werkstätte had taken over from the **Secession** as the leading Viennese arts and crafts organization and was employing over a hundred workers. Its work was published in journals such as *Deutsche Kunst und Dekoration* and *The Studio,* and reached a wider audience through the staging of Wiener Werkstätte exhibitions (Berlin 1904, Vienna & Brünn 1905, Hagen 1906) and through participatoin in various international

Dagobert Peche, poster for the fashion division of the Wiener Werkstätte, 1920

↓**Josef Hoffmann,** cut-glass vase produced by Ludwig Moser & Söhne for the Wiener Werkstätte, c. 1920

Josef Hoffmann,
silver teapot for the
Wiener Werkstätte,
1903–1904

→ **Josef Hoffmann,**
silver vase with glass
liner for the Wiener
Werkstätte, 1906

exhibitions such as the 1914 Cologne "Werkbund-Ausstellung" and the 1925 Paris "Exposition Internationale des Arts Décoratifs". Between 1903 and 1932, the Werkstätte produced furniture, glassware, metalware, textiles, jewellery, clothing, wallpapers, **ceramics** and graphics by over two hundred designers (many of whom had studied at the Kunstgewerbeschule in Vienna), including Otto Prutscher, Jutta Sika, Michael Powolny, Carl Otto Czeschka, Berthold Löffler and Emmanuel Josef Margold. The Werkstätte also undertook three notable **Gesamtkunstwerk** projects: their own theatre, the Cabaret Fledermaus (1907), Josef Hoffmann's Purkersdorf Sanatorium (1904–1906) and the Palais Stoclet (1905–1911). This latter building in Brussels exemplified the Werkstätte's early Secessionist style, which was characterized by severe rectilinearism, elaborate constructions and luxury materials. After Fritz Wärndorfer's emigration to America in 1914, the Werkstätte, managed by their new sponsor Otto Primavesi, began to produce less exclusive products that were more curvilinear and stylistically eclectic and were typified by the work by Dagobert Peche. Although branches were established in New York and Berlin in 1921 and 1929 respectively, the Wiener Werkstätte was forced into liquidation in 1932.

| Biographies | Charlotte Fiell studied at the British Institute, Florence, and at Camberwell School of Arts & Crafts, London, where she received a BA (Hons.) in the History of Drawing and Printmaking with Material Science. She later trained with Sotheby's Institute, also in London. |

Peter Fiell trained with Sotheby's Institute in London and later received an MA in Design Studies from Central St Martin's College of Art & Design, London.

Charlotte and Peter Fiell are leading authorities on 20th and 21st-century design and have written numerous books on the subject, including Taschen's *1000 Lights, 1000 Chairs, Design of the 20th Century, Industrial Design A-Z, Scandinavian Design, Designing the 21st Century* and *Graphic Design for the 21st Century*. Together they work from London as Taschen's international design book editors-in-charge. They also run a design consultancy specializing in the sale, acquisition, study and promotion of design artifacts.

The Fiells can be contacted at p.fiell@taschen.com.

Acknowledgements We would like to take this opportunity to thank all at Taschen for the successful realization of yet another project, especially our editor Viktoria Hausmann. Special thanks must also go to our editorial consultant, Thomas Berg, and to our research assistant, Quintin Coville. We are also enormously grateful to the many individuals, manufacturers, distributors, design offices, auction houses, public institutions and picture libraries who have lent their assistance and provided images. Thanks must also go to Paul Chave for his excellent new photography.

Special thanks to:

A&E Design, Stockholm
Advanced Vehicle Design, Altrincham
AEG Aktiengesellschaft, Frankfurt
Alessi, Crusinallo
Animal, Wareham
Artek, Helsinki
Atomic, Altenmarkt
Barry Friedman Ltd., New York
Biro Bic Ltd., London
Braun GmbH, Kronberg im Taunus
Callaway Golf Europe, Chessington
Cooper-Hewitt Museum, New York
Daimler-Chrysler, Detroit
Design Research Unit, London
Ecco Design, New York
Electrolux, Stockholm
Fiat UK, Slough
Fischer Fine Art, Vienna
Ford Motor Company, Brentwood
Frazer Designers, London
General Motors Corp., Detroit
Giugiaro Design, Moncalieri
Haslam & Whiteway, London
Honda UK Ltd., Reading
IBM Corp., Armonk
Imperial War Museum, London

Knoll International, New York
Lewis Moberley, London
London Transport Museum, London
Ross & Miska Lovegrove, London
Motivation, Bristol
Museé des Arts Décoratifs de Montreal
Die Neue Sammlung, Munich
Nissan Motor Co., Tokyo
NPK Industrial Design, Leiden
Pentagram Design, London
Pethick & Money Ltd., London
Raymond Loewy International, London
Remarkable Pencils Ltd., London
Science & Society Picture Library, London
Seymour Powell, London
Shimano Europe, Nunspeet
Silhouette International, Linz
Smart Cars UK, London
Sotheby's Picture Library, London
Torsten Bröhan, Berlin
Toshiba Corp., Tokyo
Volvo Corp., Gotenburg
Vitra GmbH, Weil am Rhein
The Wedgwood Museum, Barlaston
The Wolfsonian (FIU), Miami
Zanotta, Milan

Picture Credits

We are immensely grateful to those individuals and institutions who have allowed us to reproduce images. We would also like to thank the numerous designers, manufacturers and institutions who have kindly supplied images. The publisher has endeavoured to respect the rights of third parties and if any rights have been overlooked in individual cases, the mistake will be correspondingly amended where possible. The majority of the historical images were sourced from the authors' own picture archive.

A&E Design: 72 (top), 72 (bottom) – A. H. Heineken: 78 (bottom) – Advanced Vehicle Design: 55 (top) – AEG: 64 (bottom), 169 – Alessi: 60, 143 (left), 143 (right),150, 151, 168 – Animal: 77 (bottom right) – Artek: 130, 144 (top) – Atomic: 77 (left) – Audi: 9 – Avocet: 77 (bottom left) – B&B Italia: 147 – Braun GmbH: 101 – Torsten Bröhan: 11, 34, 47, 63 (top), 63 (bottom), 90 (top), 100 (bottom), 103 (top), 124 (bottom), 186 – Barry Friedman Limited: 23, 25, 39, 40, 45, 46, 50, 67, 69, 104 (top), 109, 124 (top), 163, 179 (bottom), 185, 187 – Fred Baier: 66 (top) – Biro Bic Ltd.: 138 (top), 138 (bottom) – Callaway Golf Europe: 76 (bottom) – Carrera: 55 (bottom) – Casio: 112 (bottom) – Cassina SpA: 105 – Cathers & Dembrosky: 33 – Cooper-Hewitt Museum: 37, 58 (bottom – photo: Dave King) – DaimlerChrysler: 171 – Design Council (Millennium Products): 71 (bottom), 74 (bottom right), 76 (top) – Design Research Unit: 166 (top) – Die Neue Sammlung: 132 (photo: Angela Bröhan), 141 (left – photo: Angela Bröhan), 141 (right – photo: Angela Bröhan), 146 (photo: Angela Bröhan) – Draenert: 149 (bottom) – Ecco Design: 83 – Electrolux: 59 (bottom) – Fiat: 167 (bottom) – Fiell International Limited (photo: Paul Chave): 15, 48 (top), 100 (top), 113 (top), 134 (top), 134 (bottom), 144 (bottom), 161, 169 (bottom) – Fischer Fine Art: 48 (bottom), 125, 145, 182 (bottom), 183 – Ford Motor Company: 87 (top), 87 (bottom), 88, 89 – Fortunato Depero Museum: 92, 93 – Frazer Designers: 167 (top) – Giugiaro Design: 77 (right top) – Haslam & Whiteway: 29, (The Birkenhead Collection): 10 – Zaha Hadid: 70 – IBM: 61 – Imperial War Museum: 119 (bottom), 120, 121 – Knoll International: 106 – Kunstgewerbemuseum, Berlin: 61 (photo: Saturia Linke) – Lewis Moberley: 644 – Luxo Italiana: 149 (top) – John Makepeace: 66 (bottom) – McDonald's Restaurants Ltd.: 53 – Memphis: 115 (top), 116, 118 – Michael Hopkins & Partners: 97 (photo: Tim Street-Porter) – Motivation: 78 (top) – Museé des Arts Décoratifs de Montreal: 35 (photo: Schecter Lee) – Néotu: 165 – N.P.K. (Ninaber, Peters, Krouwel): 166 (bottom) – OMK: 12 (top) – Nissan: 158 (top) – Pentagram: 59 (top) – Pethick & Money Ltd.: 137 – Protector Technologies: 74 (bottom-left) – Race Furniture: 12 (bottom) – Random Technologies: 71 (top) – Raymond Loewy International: 64 (top), 65, 174 – Remarkable Pencils Ltd.: 82 (bottom) – Ron Arad Associates: 148 – Sanderson & Sons: 28 – Science & Society Picture Library: 52 (bottom), 56 (bottom), 74 (top), 113 (bottom), 159, 160 (bottom), 160 (top) – Seymour Powell: 57 – Shimano: 13 – Silhouette: 112 (top) – Smart Cars UK: 123 – Smart Design: 73 (left), 73 (right) – Sotheby's: 30, 31, 115 (bottom), 155 (bottom), 156, 176 – Stelton: 142 – Stokke: 84 (bottom) – Stuart Parr Gallery: 129 – Tim Street-Porter: 94–95 – Studio Alchimia: 10 – Studio X – Ross Lovegrove (photo: John Ross): 85 (top), 85 (bottom), 86, 130, 133, 154 – Taschen GmbH: 24 (top), 24 (bottom), 38, 41, 43, 44, 79, 81, 90 (bottom), 98, 110, 112, 173 (top), 173 (bottom), 181 (right) – Toshiba Corp.: 82 (top), 114 – UPI/Bettmann Archive: 102 – Vitra GmbH: 155 (top) – Volvo Corp.: 75 – The Wedgwood Museum: 56 (top) – The Wolfsonian – Florida International University, The Michell Wolfson Jr. Collection: 36 (top), 135 – Yamaha: 158 (bottom) – Zanotta: 18, 20

To stay informed about upcoming TASCHEN titles, please request our magazine
at www.taschen.com/magazine or write to TASCHEN America, 6671 Sunset Boulevard,
Suite 1508, USA-Los Angeles, CA 90028, contact-us@taschen.com, Fax: +1-323-463.4442.
We will be happy to send you a free copy of our magazine which is filled with information
about all of our books.

Front Cover: Eero Aarnio, *Pastille* armchair for Asko, 1967–1968
Back Cover: Josef Hoffmann, silver vase with glass liner for the Wiener Werkstätte, 1906

Design: Sense/Net, Andy Disl and Birgit Reber and Claudia Frey, Cologne
Coordination: Viktoria Hausmann and Thomas Berg, Cologne
Production: Ute Wachendorf, Cologne

Printed in Italy
ISBN 3–8228–4633–3

Graphic Design for the 21st Century
Charlotte & Peter Fiell /
Flexi-cover, 640 pp. / € 29.99 /
$ 39.99 / £ 19.99 / ¥ 5.900

TASCHEN'S 1000 Favourite Websites
Ed. Julius Wiedemann / Flexi-cover,
book + DVD / 608 pp. / € 29.99 /
$ 39.99 / £ 19.99 / ¥ 5.900

Industrial Design
Charlotte & Peter Fiell /
Flexi-cover, 192 pp. / € 6.99 /
$ 9.99 / £ 4.99 / ¥ 1.500

"These books are beautiful objects, well-designed and lucid." —*Le Monde*, Paris, on the ICONS series

"Buy them all and add some pleasure to your life."